PRAISE FOR
LOVING SCOT

"A mother's deeply loving tribute to her talented, charismatic son. From the glamour of the disco tinged 70's into the drag world and through an exploration of dual addictions, *Loving Scott* is a mother and son's complex, symbiotic relationship—heartfelt, raw and compelling."
—Marlene Adelstein, author of *USA Today* Bestseller, *Sophie Last Seen*

"This intriguing and moving memoir of a mother's journey raising a 'different drummer' son several decades ago is more timely now than ever."
—Debbie Seaman, *The Fearless Flier's Handbook*

"Pat is an excellent writer and the story is so interesting."
—Abigail Thomas, *A Three Dog Life*

"You gave me a gift. I had been struggling at a low point and your story was what I needed. It gave me what my son needed to hear—that I am already proud of him. Your heart has helped me."
—Carol Cadmus, editor, *Peloton Advantage*

"Visual Artist Pat Horner's memoir of her talented son is a loving remembrance of his storied career as an international performance artist working the New York and Paris avant-garde scenes. Beautiful, creative and successful, Scott is portrayed by his mother with great sensitivity and at times, pain. The memoir is a must read for anyone who has lost a treasured child too early."
—Martha Ellen Hughes, author, *Precious in His Sight*, Viking/Penguin; Bennington College MFA grad; NYU creative writing teacher, founder of Peripatetic Writing Workshop, Inc.

"Scott's Story is the heart-breaking reveal of an outstanding drag queen lost too early to drugs and alcohol. It is also the story of his artist mother, only 18 when he was born, overwhelmed by motherhood and prone to escape into whatever she could find. And it is a crystal clear reflection of deep love and grief for a precious lost son, who defied convention and triumphed by living true to his nature."

—Maureen Brady, *Getaway, Ginger's Fire, Folly, Give Me Your Good Ear, The Question She Put to Herself, Daybreak: Meditations for Women Survivors of Sexual Abuse and Midlife Meditations*, and *Beyond Survival*. She teaches creative writing at NYU and The Peripatetic Writing Workshop.

LOVING SCOTT

A MEMOIR

PAT HORNER

Epigraph Books
Rhinebeck, New York

Loving Scott: A Memoir Copyright © 2023 by Pat Horner

All rights reserved. No part of this book may be used or reproduced in any manner without the consent of the author except in critical articles or reviews. Contact the publisher for information.

This book is a memoir. It reflects the author's present recollections of experiences over time. To protect privacy some names and characteristics have been changed, some events have been compressed, and some dialog has been recreated.

Hardcover ISBN 978-1-960090-08-9
Paperback ISBN 978-1-960090-09-6
eBook ISBN 978-1-960090-10-2

Library of Congress Control Number 2023904451

Book design by Colin Rolfe

Epigraph Books
22 East Market Street, Suite 304
Rhinebeck, NY 12572
(845) 876-4861
epigraphps.com

CONTENTS

Prologue ix

PART I.
Growth

1	On Death and Ghosts	3
2	Baby Blanket	7
3	Veils	9
4	Beginning: 1950–1963	15
5	Learning to Walk	21
6	Minneapolis	25
7	Entrepreneurship	31
8	Expanding	35
9	Finding Identity	39
10	Productions and Performances	43
11	Flo and Freedom	47
12	Sex Education	51
13	Graduate School and Jerry Garcia	55
14	Pittsburgh	67
15	New York City	75
16	Frog Dream	81
17	Return to Minneapolis	85
18	Failure at Motherhood	89
19	Another Mentor	91
20	Trip to Miami	97
21	Recovery and Addiction	101

PART II.
Light

22	Sober in New York City	125
23	Why Dress Up?	129

24	Drag	135
25	Love Addiction	139
26	East Village Drag	147
27	Paris	151
28	Berlin and Fame	155
29	Professional Beginnings	159
30	Meeting Jed	163
31	Relationships	167
32	Kevyn and Technique	171
33	A Memory	175
34	The Castle	177
35	Jezebel	181
36	The Breakup	185
37	A Feeling	189

PART III.
Afterlife

38	Saying Goodbye	195
39	Life Mask	199
40	The Makeup Case	215
41	Orchids	217
42	Scott's Things and Ring	221
43	Legacy	225
44	Last Meal	231
45	Letting Go	235
46	Acceptance	239
47	Coming Out of Denial	243
48	Becoming Part of Me	247

Epilogue: Looking Back	251
Acknowledgments	257
About the Author	259

LOVING SCOTT

Nan Goldin with Misdemeanor and friend.
Paris, 1991, Photos by author (PA)

PROLOGUE

Paris, 1991:

Spring arrived late and cafes on the Right Bank put tables out on the sidewalks. My son Scott and I both loved Paris, with its narrow streets, terraces, and friendly faces. A city that honored women, whose images appeared on French francs, both paper and coins, stamps, posters, and statues enshrined on monuments in parks, on buildings and bridges. They represented freedom, equality, reason. The city was also a refuge for drag performers and artists. Since the jazz days of Josephine Baker, the French had adopted avant-garde artists who wanted to escape from the cruelty toward the different, the unusual, or unique.

In 1991 photographer Nan Goldin scheduled an opening at the new Bastille Opera House in Paris. She would be exhibiting her photographic/sound performance, *Ballad of Sexual Dependency*, projecting color slides of her extended family, including young drag queens from New York that made her famous. Nan invited Scott to perform as "Miss Demeanor," to open the show with a drag performance on stage. He shopped the New York vintage and thrift shops for days to find the perfect outfit—a short, curly, pink/blond wig; long, sparkly earrings; a ritzy, silver-lamé, turtlenecked, sleeveless top—tight over the perfectly sized falsies; a long-contoured, beige-and-black jersey skirt; and long black gloves covered in large teardrop rhinestones. I wore boots; tights; a short, gathered wool skirt; and a leather jacket—all black.

LOVING SCOTT

Scott and Nan were staying in the Marais, a hip district near the center of Paris, close to where I lived. I joined them at the before-party of celebrities and artists at photographer Betina Rhemes's home on the Rue St. Antoine. A few of us walked the several blocks to the Bastille, picking up tourists, gawkers, or late-coming friends along the way. My son, as a beautiful woman in four-inch heels, towering over us all, strutted as only a drag queen could. I ran ahead of the group to document the scene with my M2 Leica camera as men and women on the street turned in wonder and respect. I was a photographer and that evening felt more a proud mother honored to be associated with this gathering of rebels and nonconformists.

The Opera House was half filled with young gays, artists, photographers, and Nan's fans. Her fame had reached beyond New York City. Music blared as Scott went backstage. I was seated on the aisle, close to the stage, as I requested, though I had not been given permission to photograph his big break. This was the life my son had chosen, and I wanted him to live it with my blessing and approval. The lights went down in hushed chatter and Scott, as Miss Demeanor, walked on the stage and greeted the packed audience with her perfectly pronounced *"Bonsoir,"* addressing us before lip syncing her opening number, "Non, Je ne Regrette Rien,"–No, I don't regret anything. I was giddy with excitement at his presentation of the Edith Piaf song.

Scott appeared to give off sparks while seducing us to manifest our own fantasies. With perfect movements, he sauntered from one side of the stage to the other, captivating the audience with a thoroughly professional show. A smile was etched on my face as I snuck a few photos. After his performance of a dozen songs by Lena Horn, Madeline Kahn, Dinah Washington, and other world-famous female singers, there were standing ovations and requests for two encores. The applause reminded me of the home performances he did years before in our South Minneapolis house. My son was now making a living from the games of his childhood, playing out past performances of an inner female.

Backstage, Scott was excited, surrounded by Nan, a few friends, and me.

"Are there reporters out there? Did you get some good photos of me on stage? I would have done more, but I thought I should only perform the ones I practiced. Besides, it's better to leave them wanting more—don't you think? I didn't want the audience to be *too* satisfied." He smiled at me as he had so often in childhood, with pride. Scott was at home in this world of nonconformity.

His other drag persona, "Misty," usually seemed to be more fun for Scott to perform—he loved the younger, scuzzier side to her—yet Miss Demeanor was his more "professional" persona, demanding the serious and proper appreciation of her beholders. "Miss Demeanor" also got paid better and was more akin to the new Scott, no longer a relic from the days of Midwestern, conservative conformity where one does what everyone else does—run from controversy, hide in a tight-box, close-the-lid-and-tape-it-shut kind of place. And now, Scott was wearing high heels. He wasn't able to run to, or from, anything.

After the performance, several of us went to a nearby restaurant where a table was set for thirty or more in the back room. There were queer folks, artists, agents, publishers, writers, and photographers all crowded together, many whom I knew or wanted to know.

I was having an exhibit of my own photographic collage work in Paris at the time. But this was Scott's night, and I would not poach on Nan or her new international star, Miss Demeanor. We were a gathering of misfits, a rare combination of originality, authenticity, and courage—forming friendships or connections for the decade ahead, one that many of us believed would be friendlier to gays and others like us. We all wanted new freedoms.

* * *

Willow, New York, 2016—twenty-five years later:
Outside, the wrens were calling each other, chirping messages I could only guess at—*Bring food. Hawk flying in on left. Find fluff for nest.* I was sitting in my own nest in the back bedroom of the house in Willow, New York, a hamlet of Woodstock, that my husband David and I bought in 1995.

That ranch house, on a shaded road eight miles from the town's Village Green, between a stream and a field that was once a farm, is still home to us. Our bedroom has a large picture window and another smaller, square window above. A Buddha resting on the sill looks out over the room and on that day smiled at me as I tried to make sense of my loss. Our cat Izzy purred on the bed, sinking into the down comforter until I could see only her ear and fat tummy. The morning sunlight dappled the room, my sanctuary, flooding over the plush sofa where I reclined on large pillows.

A Shaker-style bed, good for conjuring dreams and restoring energy, was my haven from the mad rush of trains and buses, cars, and sirens screeching during my visit to New York City over the past three days. Older artwork on the white walls held peaceful colors and shapes under glass and reminded me of the deeper, sweeter depths to living, to being. I had the fluff and food I needed while I watched carefully for the hawk outside.

The lack of new art on the walls was a reminder of how little I'd accomplished since my son had passed at age fifty, when I was sixty-eight; of how empty the space and my existence had become. The only life in the room was Izzy, our fat black cat, and an older artist/writer attempting to find words that would mean something.

As the evening light dimmed, my image of Scott started to fade away. I called out, "Come back!" Coldness swept in as the clouds outside grew dark. He appeared again with deep wounds on his face, the ones I remembered from the dark brown and green decomposed image of him on the TV monitor at the medical examiner's office. He'd been photographed when he was found

PROLOGUE

by police, five days after his death. He died from bleeding out. I imagined my son's body lying in a pool of blood on a cold tile floor in his Long Island City apartment, between the kitchen and living room, near a shattered glass, which he must have reached for before his fall.

The next day my husband David and I were allowed to go into the apartment for twenty minutes to retrieve important papers, keys, checkbook, and anything else needed to help prove our identity and relationship to Scott. I rushed around the dried bloody spot where his body had lain and opened the balcony door to air out five days of death. Stepping onto the balcony, I took a deep breath and wept silently into loud traffic below as I wiped my eyes and grabbed a few orchids that would need watering.

Back home in the tranquility of my bedroom, I listened to the birds' sweet whistling, the crows' cawing, and the wind softly blowing. The oak, maple, and beech trees outside were so alive, having come out of rocks, pushing energy towards the light, towards heaven. I thought of my son standing tall and proud, as beautiful as the trees.

How am I to describe the inspiration he gave me while being in my life and stimulating so many others along his way? His calm smile, heart, and soul were beacons that lit the way to a more creative, authentic life. While others were busy in the reality of their daily lives, Scott appeared to be somewhere else; he seemed to touch the sky with a youthful, uncharted curiosity—listening to grace, wanting more.

Come with me, I'll take you there, I heard him say, melting us with his loving nature and sweet personality. Throughout childhood and his careers in the New York drag scene and makeup business, Scott stayed humble and grounded. He connected instantly to people while he wove through the cruel homophobia of society and the bravado and craziness of the fashion world.

Having done little artwork or writing for years since the day my son was found dead, I finally wrote for hours, trying to find words that would bring to life my memories of his nature. As the room became darker, Scott's form appeared, face puffy from the drug he was taking to cure the hepatitis C virus he carried. His hair bleached white, wearing an old, olive-green, cashmere sweater over torn blue jeans. Smelling of smoke and alcohol.

"What are you doing?" he asked.

"Trying to put your life on a page," I answered.

He chuckled. "Why? No one cares." There was an uncomfortable feeling in the room, as if large, heavy hands were pushing me down.

"I care!!—And I want to share your life with others," I said, crying as he backed away and faded into the air. A blanket of gloom descended over me. My expectations came in to fill the space with thoughts of guilt and judgements I'd held for the past fifty years of my son's life. I wanted no more imagination or inspiration, only a concrete understanding of him that I feared I would never have.

I remembered a mild fall day at my mother's house. Scott was a happy, curious, adorable, two-year-old watching colorful leaves dancing around him. Dressed in navy-blue shorts and a blue and white shirt, running through piles of leaves, smiling and laughing, stopping only to pose for my camera when I called his name. Scott was masquerading, as he later did in drag as Misty for Nan Goldin. He began his career at two years old, a sailor navigating into an identity.

Scott often looked up to me for direction, or perhaps to examine my face. In a picture from my mother's house that day, he was climbing up her outside steps to be closer to me. Was he studying my makeup like the times later, when he joined me in the bathroom to watch while I got ready for a night out. He stood on the closed toilet seat inspecting me, searching intently as he gazed at me, then the mirror. He picked up my lipstick, opened it carefully, and held it towards my lips.

"Why are you staring at me?" I'd ask.

"See you paint," he'd answered.

PROLOGUE

I suspected he was gay early on when he was so sensitive, gentle, and attached to the monkey-faced bear his grandmother had given him. He held it like his own baby while Bob, his father, wanted to throw it away. After Scott died, I found it in a box in his apartment, hidden with old letters and drawings.

It's as if he'd said, "I thought you could use this." I imagined him handing me his box filled with words and images that would help me piece together his life, a wonderful yet troubled span of only fifty years.

The bear is now in my box of memories, next to a picture of Scott's friends, their four backs to the camera as they bow on their knees, two with bare backs and wide-rim hats, one in drag. They prayed in front of the memorial table that held the framed photo of Scott's smiling face, a lit candle next to the photo on one side, a large white orchid on the other. In the box is also a copy of his obituary, one column condensing an entire life, so short, yet more than most drag performers or makeup artists get.

Scott's life was filled with heartache, competition, but also success. Love, and enough money to buy the expensive things he so fiercely desired. Cultivated from his taste for the best, always the best. Through a rapid roller coaster of social restrictions and limits, through sadness and pain, he accomplished an incredible amount of work. The proof is on pages that now live in four large boxes stuffed with magazine tear sheets of pretty women, all made more beautiful by my son. They were lucky to be close to him, face to face. I simply wanted him back.

His interests were many: orchids, gardening, astronomy, cooking, music—especially classical, playing his Steinway baby grand for hours. Any subject was enlightened by his perceptions, and though he excelled in most classes, school became limiting for him.

"I got an A in drawing," he said when I asked about his classes at the Minneapolis College of Art and Design. By his second year his patience had run the course, and Bs and Cs in classes other than Art were unacceptable to him. He dropped out.

No longer satisfied by conceiving him in my imagination when I felt strong, on the days when the sun was out and the sadness was kept at bay, I wanted so much to see him again—alive, smiling, teasing me as he often did. After Scott passed, I had little or no desire for the life I knew. Nothing seemed important. Escape lured me, but as I waited for something, anything to alleviate that sick, deep feeling of dark clouds outside the window, I was reminded by the ever-occurring sun that life would go on, and so should I.

Misdemeanor with Nan, friend
and Jack Pierson, PA

PART I.

Growth:

* * *

The Black-Lipped Orchid, *Coelogyne pandurate.*
Apple green epiphyte found on large trees.
Almost always in a state of active growth.

Scott with his sister Kim. Minneapolis,
c. 1966 – 1970, PA

CHAPTER ONE

ON DEATH AND GHOSTS

"Why do people die?" Scott asked me in 1968, when he was five. I was taking laundry out from the clothes dryer in the basement between his playroom and my darkroom.

"All living things die," I answered after a lengthy pause while folding his sister Kim's diapers. His father's cousin served two tours in the military and had recently driven head on into a semitruck with his Volkswagen. It was ruled a suicide. Scott was not at the funeral but was old enough to grasp what the Vietnam War was doing to so many young men. The TV was on every night.

I got down on my knees to his level and looked straight in the eyes of my only son. "Plants die, insects die and animals die. Remember when Panther died?" Our sixteen-year-old cat had been found dead under the coffee table a few weeks earlier. "And people die," I whispered. I thought of how my grandmother looked as she lay dying on the hospital bed in her dining room when I was twelve.

"But normally people die when they are very old and sick." I offered this as someone who was serving cheese and crackers might say, "Hungry? Have some of these."

"How old was he?" Scott's large eyes looked up at me when we returned upstairs. He was always asking questions, many of which perplexed me but also taught me patience and inspiration. At times he became my rescuer from a mundane housewife's existence.

"Twenty-three," I answered, "and that's why we're so sad." I thought of my father's death, hoping Scott could grasp this concept better than I had at age sixteen. I didn't know what else I could say. Now, decades later and in hindsight, I imagine I could have explained it better by showing him the wooden bowl that was always present in every home I had lived in since leaving my mother's house.

I *could* have told him that our lives are like this bowl, exquisitely carved, hand turned, molded into a beautiful work of art, made from a log of a once living tree. It will last perhaps seventy or eighty years or more, but then will return to nature, as we all do. The roundness and imperfections are part of its beauty, its uniqueness, and remind us that cycles or lives are not always how we mean them to be. The bowl is part of the earth, nothing more.

Instead, I promised my son, "You won't die for a long, long time."

Years later, I looked at the rounded carved wooden globe on the bookcase that Scott gave me one year for my birthday. The size of a small bowling ball, it cannot be used as a vase except for a few dried flowers. Water would ruin the precious wood and the hole is too small for more than perhaps two or three small stems. I picked up the globe—entombed in worm holes, cracks and veins, transformed into a thing of beauty—and was reminded of nature. The scent of newly carved wood that it held when he gave it to me is now gone but the remnants of the tree remain. The lines and scars recount the life it, and Scott, had for fifty years. I try to find solace in that.

Scott's fear of the dead started the same year, when he heard knocking at the attic door across from his room. He ran to whisper in my ear, "Somebody's upstairs." I had never seen him so frightened and suggested he go with me to see. He hovered on the stairway unable to go further as I searched every corner.

"Is it ghosts?" he asked, recently having seen *Topper* on TV.

"Maybe," I answered, "But if it is, for sure, they're friendly."

I explained to him how good it was to have "spirits" around us, keeping watch and making us safe. Convinced by my assurance, he slept soundly that night.

A few years later, on Halloween, Scott chose to be a ghost. It was one of his favorite holidays. Each year he would begin weeks ahead to plan a horror house in the garage. Asking for grapes and a bowl of cooked spaghetti one day, I wondered if he had had enough lunch and asked where he was taking them.

"To my horror house. It's a surprise." Our garage had a large hole, a pit built for working on cars from underneath. Scott borrowed a shopping cart from the market and took the smaller kids down a ramp into the total darkness of the pit, handing them bowls of "snacks". After they ate, Scott turned on the flashlight and told the terrified children the peeled grapes and spaghetti were the eyeballs and guts of the dead person. He had fabricated the body from old clothing stuffed with leaves, and painted red as if blood had spattered from knife wounds.

He loved frightening them and continued even into his last Halloween, where pictures on Instagram show him on the subway with several friends in costumes. Scott was dressed as a tuxedoed man, a hatchet in his head and blood running down his face. Ghosts and horror films became an obsession for him, even though death was kept filed away somewhere else. He never went to funerals or visited relatives or friends who were dying yet seemed to make friends with ghosts whenever he heard or saw something strange.

* * *

I awoke one day, long after his death, smelling argan oil, which Scott used to keep his dry, static hair from flying about. As I looked around and wondered if it was a dream, I thought, "Where are you now?"

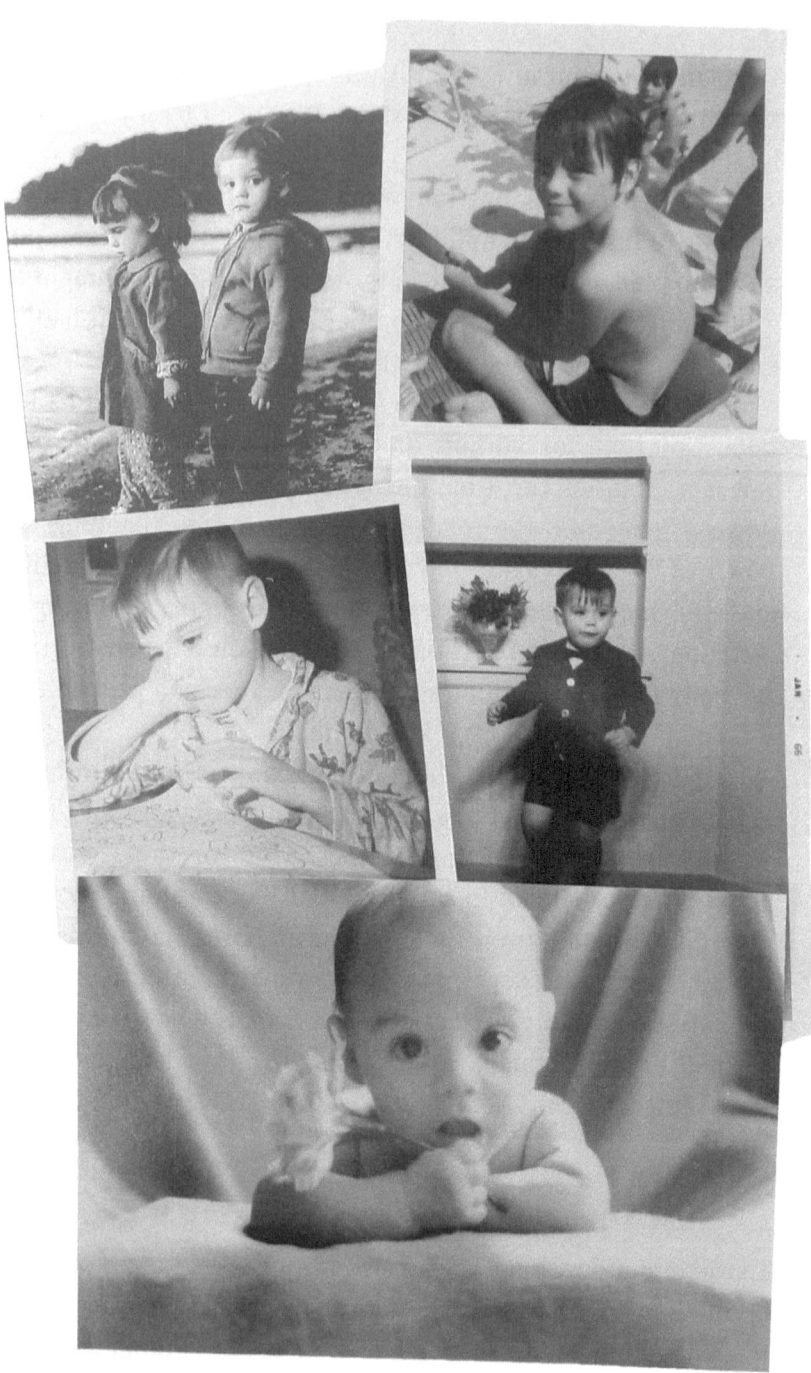

Cousin Sandy with Scott.
c. 1964 - 1970, PA

CHAPTER TWO

BABY BLANKET

Our home in Willow has a second-story meditation room designed and built by David, my architect husband. After Scott's death, I often went up there to read, or sleep, or contemplate Scott's life. In a dream one day, a delicate scent of sweet pea drifted in as Scott levitated in a vast house with no ceiling. He looked as though he had not finished dressing: in half drag, in his everyday casual white sleeveless shirt and a short pink crinoline skirt hemmed with sparkling silver edges. He wore knee-high shiny black patent leather stiletto boots, partially hiding seamed net stockings. Scott had on his short, neon-sky-blue wig, and with a lit cigarette in his hand his quirky smile was unbearably sweet to me. He filled the room with a transparent lightness.

"Don't forget to add three things to my story," he said.

I looked around for pen and paper as his image faded, evaporating into the blurring wall behind him. I awoke trying hard to recall, searching the dusty corners of my brain for what he'd said, or what I wanted to say. I was hoping he'd return to remind me.

Later I remembered the blue comforter that someone gave Scott at birth. He continuously sucked on the corners of the blanket for two years, crying when I took it away to wash. While he napped, I repaired the frayed corners, cutting and sewing each until the blanket was round. I read Dr. Spock, who interpreted the sucking as a need for a sense of security or to build self-esteem, a way to say, "I can do for myself."

When Scott was born in 1963, gays hid in closets, afraid, hiding their true selves. In downtown Minneapolis, aside from Augie's drag bar, there was little sign of anything beyond an Ozzie and Harriet lifestyle. No unconventional families, no drug abuse. If you knew a gay or a "fag," you kept quiet since "knowing" usually came from being around young men hanging outside of Augie's, dressed in tight jeans with one leg up against the wall, smoking a cigarette, sizing up each man who entered. You might be labeled as one who wraps their life in veils and mystery, hiding behind a demon, bound in the complex history of their own family. In other words, a degenerate. Some male friends knew of these conflicted young "lost souls" and were quick to point out Scott's traits.

"He's wearing lipstick!" our neighbor exclaimed when Scott was three years old.

"Why does he put on his mother's clothes?" a friend's husband asked me. I silently crossed both off my invitation list.

"She gave him a *doll*?" Bob inquired after his mother visited for Scott's fourth birthday.

A few nights later, again in a dream, Scott returned out of a shadowed nowhere, posing in full drag; a black leather bustier with a white skull-and-crossbones over a luminous pale pink, see-through, long-sleeved, sparkly tulle top. Underneath, a black bra over well-formed falsies. His face was fully made up with ruby red lips, black mascara, eyeliner and eyebrows, huge hooped dangling rhinestone earrings.

"Did you remember?" my son asked.

"Of course!" I really wasn't sure whether my memories of the blanket, Augie's, and the doll were those he'd wanted but felt certain I would eventually recall more, and even if I didn't, it would be okay. In my mind, I was hugging him, hoping for happiness in his next life.

CHAPTER THREE

VEILS

Weeks later, Scott appeared in another dream with a puffy face, again with the drug-altered look he had at the end of his life. His hair was bleached white and he was wearing his black-rimmed Gucci glasses, torn blue jeans, and an old orange and brown torn sweater with a Friends of Bonaparte insignia on the front. He smelled of smoke and alcohol and asked, "What are you doing?"

"I'm still writing about you," I answered.

He laughed. "Am I your subject now?" my son asked with a half-crooked smile. It was the same smile he had when he was seven, dressed in my senior prom gown, and the smile he gave me when I first showed up at Wigstock to see him as a drag performer. Since that day, the playful smile had gone from sheepishly demure to completely confident as he became a makeup artist who got paid to do what he loved.

"Yes. Right now, my art is sharing your talents with others," I answered. I was reliving the past fifty years of feelings around the idea of my son putting on women's clothes. It had seemed to some others that he wanted to be a woman, but I believed he just liked dressing up.

Being transgender isn't a matter of simply dressing in different clothes. It has little to do with doing drag. Crossdressers or transvestites take their identity very seriously. Their identity is who they are. It's permanent. They dress up for psychological needs.

Drag queens dress up for entertainment. They are simply playing.

Ru Paul said, "Drag is really making fun of identity. We are shapeshifters. We're like okay, today I'm this, now I'm a cowboy, now I'm this. . . . I come from the school of I will do whatever I want to do, at any time, and change—whatever!"

Drag queens were called *pantomime dames* in late nineteenth-century Europe. The first drag balls in the US were performed by slaves in Washington DC during the 1880s.

In 2015, a year after Scott passed, *Drag Queen Story Hour* was launched at the San Francisco Public Library, followed in 2016 in Brooklyn, then traveled to libraries, museums, bookstores, recreation centers, and parks across the US, Canada, and the United Kingdom. Though these events have prompted opposition, they have also inspired young people to be more authentic.

A parent's journey is to accept a child who is different. Many have to deal with a gay son or daughter but others have the extra element of having a son who wants to dress up and perform in drag. I let Scott be who he was. When conflict arose between his father and me, it did not in any way keep me from siding with my son. My tendency to encourage Scott by not interfering with his inclinations may have been one reason the family broke up.

Scott, drifting closer to me in my dream, was unusually serious. "But none of that matters now. My life or the past. Why not do what you taught me, to live in the present with imagination and inspiration?" Scott asked as he floated around the room, looking at my collages again.

He had learned important lessons before he could walk. While in his Johnny Jump Up watching me make dinner, he seemed curious about the spice cabinet. The next day, at 5:00 a.m. he crawled to the kitchen, pulled over a step stool to reach the upper cabinet and grabbed the pepper container. He turned it upside down, trying to see what was inside. His screams woke me to the horror an adventurous child can cause. I ran to find pepper in his eyes, on his pajamas, the counter and floor. I knew it was time to buy more toys, and locks for the cabinets.

In my dream, the smile faded from Scott's face as he pointed to a collage on the wall, a cut out of a head. Just the forehead and eyes were visible through threads hanging from the top. On the second half below, there was a gathered, see-through, beige skirt covering a photo of a tree. It was as if there was a veiled secret that would stay until the picture was unframed. The eyes were from an undifferentiated male or female, representing both.

"I still think these are what you should be working on." Scott had rarely given advice to me or anyone, often changing the subject if things got serious, a holdover from conservative Midwestern communication—do what others do—hide your feelings—pretend you don't care. He had acquired a quiet, noble gentleness after he started to live in New York City, and his friends adored Scott. Nan called him "the human valium, because he's so calm."

The idea of adding veils to my collages had started when I helped my mother and her sister, Marie, clean out their ninety-one-year-old sister Helen's apartment after she passed away. I opened a drawer filled with see-through square scarves; the ones women wore in the fifties. They were different colors, some had flowers or graphic designs printed on them. Others were simply plain blue, beige, or yellow—but all were tulle, chiffon, see through, light as a feather, and totally useless for adding warmth to the neck on a cold day. Some women used them to cover their well-coiffed hairdos, others tied up ponytails or wrapped their hats or hand bags. The scarfs were exactly what I needed to partially cover images I chose for a series of collages about AIDS in the eighties. I was losing friends and feared my once heroin-addicted son might also get it. I asked if I could have the scarfs.

"Of course!" my aunt Marie said while my mother scoffed.

"Whatever do you want those old things for?" I couldn't

explain to my mother the plans I had. I was afraid of being criticized for doing something outside the norm.

Back in my studio I put a yellow and black polka dot scarf over an illustration of a man's back, marked from some terrible disease. The image was from a thirties medical book I'd found in the library dumpster. Above the scarred image, now with its delicate 'veil', I added a picture of a factory spewing black smoke. My intent was for a viewer to be lured into the pretty scarf, hoping they would look closer, through or under the obscure covering to see the diseased man and think of either AIDS and/or pollution, the two most important subjects in my work at that time.

A few years later, while living in Paris I walked to the Pompidou and saw a book in the window of the local book store. It had the word *Mort* on the cover with an amazing black and white image of a man's head, eyes closed. I entered the shop, hoping the price was affordable. For some reason, I needed those faces.

"Ten francs?" I asked, excited to get the death masks of famous French people. I bought the book and couldn't wait to show Scott, who would soon be visiting me.

"Look what I found!" I handed him my treasure. We sat and studied the book for an hour. He was mesmerized by the faces of men he'd learned about in school.

Robespierre was my favorite. I topped his head in a pink and black polka dot scarf, like a pirate, and tied him to a dock as a train went by. Scott was amused. I liked that.

Years later, my son asked me for a special collage representing "ghosts." The next day in my studio, a frame fell from the rafters and landed at my feet. It was in dire need of refinishing but when I put an image of a floating veiled figure on a partially developed blurred photo into the frame, I knew it was the perfect piece for the ghost room. Many of his guests had told stories of noises coming from that room. Scott and I still believed that ghosts existed and traveled through time and space. They were reaffirming to us.

"I love your veiled collages," Scott often told me before and even after his death. I wondered if he was communing with those French figures from *Mort*, the death-mask book. Or did he think of them when he agreed to have his face cast into a "life" mask years later.

After his death I felt his presence when I wrapped the see-through scarves around the rough edges of the concrete-like casting of his face. I was bringing him back to life, with colored, sheer, soft, silent veils that would protect him as he slept. I imagined my mother and aunts surrounding him.

"See what magic she made!" my aunt Helen said.

"With *your* scarves!" aunt Marie exclaimed.

"And with *my* grandson," my mother whispered in my mind, pridefully. It was as though all the dead were really there, alive again.

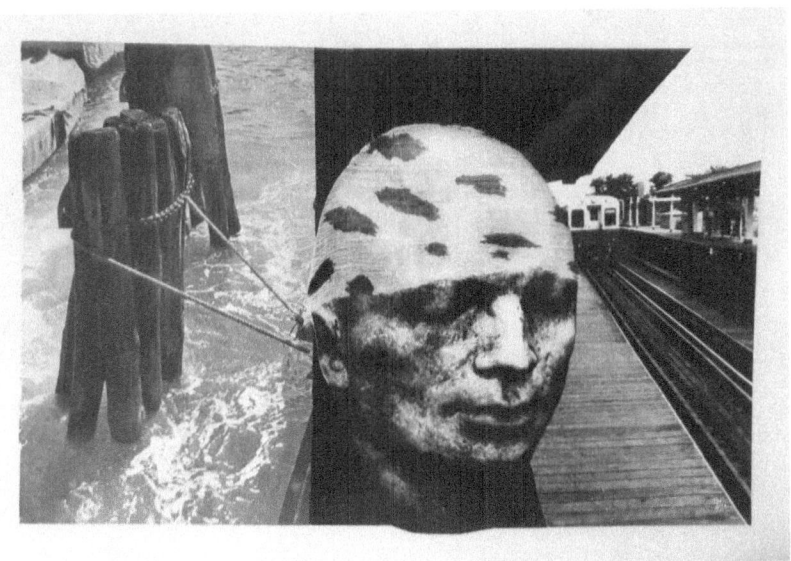

Collage, *Robespierre*, by author.

Author's brother, Tom Horner, Minneapolis, c. 1959, Photo unidentified (UNI)

CHAPTER FOUR

BEGINNING: 1950–1963

I started making art at an early age. A drawing done by my fifteen-year-old brother, Tom, when I was five, shows me in ruffled panties leaning over something. Perhaps I was painting on the floor of our two-room apartment, as I often did. My mother showed me how to trace a circle around an empty coffee can. I began drawing circles on whatever paper or cardboard I could find to paint or crayon abstract designs on. I cut each circle out and saved my works of art, piling them up before I learned that my mother threw them away each week. I still grieve those early works and use circles in collages and paintings to this day.

When I was eleven, we moved eight blocks south to a better neighborhood, across the street from the Minneapolis Institute of Art and the College of Art and Design. Going from a two-room apartment to a two-bedroom duplex was complete luxury. My older siblings, Tom and Nancy, were in college and my twelve-year-old brother, David, and I were still in grade school.

The four of us shared the largest bedroom with green plaid wallpaper, the boys on the top bunks and Nancy and I below. I was given the coveted corner nook in the bedroom because I was always doing homework, writing stories, or drawing. The nook had two large windows with northeast light and I spent many hours there when not in school. It was my only private space.

When I was fourteen, my brother Tom was twenty-four and more of a father figure to me. Our own father had become ill with alcoholism and Parkinson's. Tom gave me a German-made Retina IIIC camera with folding bellows and taught me how to use it. I took photographs of everything, climbing statues in Fair Oaks Park, a half block away or the stairs up to a Three Graces statue in the museum. I saw art everywhere and needed to document it.

Puberty flew by. There were lilac trees and generous grassy fields at the Art Institute across the street, before they built the school's art library. Any chance I had, I drew or photographed trees, my friends, old cars that my brother Tom had collected, or whatever my homework assignments suggested—insects, anatomy, world history, or current events. At times, without a subject, I made abstract designs while I started to like boys and daydreamed of growing breasts and someday having a boyfriend.

* * *

Bob Mortenson and I started dating at the beginning of tenth grade at Central High. He was tall and well-built, with beautiful brown eyes and a high forehead, like mine.

"A sign of intelligence," my father told me.

Bob was on the swim team, and I was new at the school and began to attend all the swim meets. I was happy to be liked by what seemed the most popular boy there but being a *good* girl, I didn't let any petting go too far. Kissing was okay, hugging fine—as long as his hands didn't go near my breasts or below my waist. After a few months of this, Bob exhibited frustration and began to pull away, sitting next to other girls at the ball games or parties. In February of 1961, I waited for him to come out from the lockers, as he had always done before when we had plans for the evening. The entire swim team had already gone by the time Bob's friend Steve came out to tell me Bob left with someone else.

"Who did he leave with?" I asked, tears in my eyes.

"Sue," Steve answered, lowering his head. Sue was the "hussy" of reputation and gossip.

The news spread throughout the school. I was humiliated. To be ditched was bad enough. To be ditched for a sleazy blond of ill repute was disgraceful. Weeks later Bob asked me out again. I turned him down, finding many other boys who were happy to go out with me. Although still a sophomore, I attended the senior prom with Bill, the captain of the swim team. I also began to write humorous gossip about teachers and students in a *Horner's Corner* column for the Central High School newspaper. My reputation grew. I became "popular" and dated many boys.

My first love, Dave, moved eight hours North with his family when I was sixteen. It seemed the end of the world. A few months later, my father died, and later that fall my brother Tom got married and moved out. I lost the three men I most loved, all within a few months. My father left barely enough money for a funeral. My mother started a course in nurse's training before finding out that nursing jobs paid too little to support us. After twenty-five years of being a housewife and mother, she went to work in a laundry. Nancy had married four years earlier and was living in Michigan.

Afraid and broken, I got drunk at my father's funeral. "He *was* Irish." I told myself.

Bob Mortenson continued asking me out and by the end of summer, I relented. One night after swimming in Lake Calhoun, still in our bathing suits, I began to let him put his hands under the top of my suit to touch my breasts. Soon I desired more.

We had an on-off relationship for another year before I let him go further with the petting and further still when we were seniors. By spring of 1963, a few months before graduation, we were playing with each other's genitals, removing our clothes, doing everything but intercourse, all in his bright pea green 1940 Ford coupe.

The next month, my period was late. How could I be pregnant? Had I blacked out one night? Afraid to tell anyone, I considered abortion but they were not available in the sixties—there was no pill, no alternative other than a coat hanger or an illegal back-alley operation. Unable to avoid my fear any longer, I told Bob and we made plans to get married, run off to Arizona, and start our adult lives together. We also began going all the way, as it was now clear I'd lost my virginity.

I was enrolled at the Institute of Technology at the University of Minnesota in my senior year because my grades in math and science were high, but my mother told me there was no money for college. "If you were a boy, I would find the money," she told me.

My oldest brother, Tom, twenty-seven, had graduated with an engineering degree after five years at the University of Minnesota and had a good job at the local gas company to help pay the mortgage and other household expenses. My other brother David got a job at a gas station to help, and I worked at a café/grocery store, able to save $20 a week after giving my mother $30. I was responsible for the cooking and housework but the *most* challenging job, before Tom left home, was waking him up in the morning for work. I once poured a glass of water on him. Already feeling like a housewife, running away seemed exotic. Bob and I felt like we were adults. We wanted to be away from our families and their rules. We also wanted to get away from the frigid cold of Minnesota winters.

After three weeks of planning, I awoke in a pool of blood one night and thought I'd had a miscarriage. Relieved and excited the next day, I told Bob. "Now we don't have to get married."

"Was that the only reason you were going to marry me?" he asked. What could I say to that? "No, of course not!" I lied.

We continued with our plans and, by the end of high school I still hadn't gotten my period. It had been a month since the bleeding. We left for Phoenix in the rattletrap Ford coupe two days after graduation, having left notes to our parents, knowing they would disapprove. It was the first of many geographical escapes I would attempt.

Believing my hormonal infatuation was *love*, I settled into the sixties version of being a "wife." If things went bad, at least we both had taken the responsibility. In Phoenix, Bob found a job drafting while I decorated, cooked, and cleaned in our small apartment. My period didn't come. I went to a doctor who confirmed the pregnancy and said I was due on January 8, 1964.

After four months in the Arizona summer, we hated the 100+ degree weather and felt isolated, missing friends and family. We told our parents about the pregnancy, and they urged us to move back to Minneapolis, offering to help. We drove back home in the fall and moved into my old bedroom at my mother's house. I began to think the sex had not been worth it. While I was falling out of lust, John Kennedy was assassinated. I was filled with regrets and deep sorrow, yet when Scott was born three-and-a-half weeks premature due to jaundice from our incompatible RH factor blood types, I was overjoyed. Scott Andrew Mortenson was born December 13, 1963 in Minneapolis, the city where Bob and I were born and raised. We had graduated high school only seven months before his birth. I was eighteen years old.

We brought home to my mother's house, a five-pound, wrinkled-faced baby who looked like his grandfather, an old man, but to me he was the most incredible being I had ever seen. I couldn't believe I helped create this amazing miracle.

After Scott gained weight, Bob and I moved to our own apartment near the Art Institute. Scott and I began to bond without my mother and brother around. Bob got a job, and by the spring I was taking Scott to Fair Oaks Park and the Art Institute. We strolled by the Art School that I had wanted to go to. I wondered if I would ever get there, not knowing that ten years later, I would. *For now,* I thought, *I will be content to take photographs of my son and enjoy motherhood.* Bob's parents had another plan.

Scott with his grandfather, Speed on boat.
1964, PA

CHAPTER FIVE

LEARNING TO WALK

Speed, my father-in-law, was a wiry, hard-boiled, tenacious man who owned a bar, piloted airplanes, raced cars, and was building a fifty-two-foot power boat patterned after a Chris-Craft. My mother-in-law, Dort, was a pianist. They wanted their only son to go to college and offered Scott, ten months old, and me, nineteen, an exciting trip down the river with room and board on the boat for the year. We agreed. Bob drove to Florida and started classes at a community college in Pensacola. I would stay up North with Scott until the boat was ready to dock.

We left later than planned, before a snowstorm arrived. In November 1964, Dort and I finished seventeen coats of stain on the mahogany railing and deck. The next day we launched the boat in the Mississippi River at St. Paul, Minnesota, for the trip down to Florida. Through twenty-two hundred miles and twenty-one locks, scary weather and risky adventures, we crossed the Gulf of Mexico Bay from New Orleans. Speed knew the Interstate highway bridge was going to be built from Pensacola to Avalon Beach and decided to buy property in the small gulf town. He hoped to capitalize on the commuters wanting a shorter trip to Pensacola, making the one-or-more hour car ride into less than twenty minutes.

Since Speed was colorblind, I became the navigator and photographer. Anticipating an adventure as skipper on the boat, I also thought we would escape winter, but within a few days I was on the bridge in a snowstorm spotting the red and green buoys, reading the navigation charts and watching for other boats, barges, or obstacles in the river. In the evening I was reading Lawrence Durrell's *Alexandria Quartet* and writing love letters to my first love, Dave.

Scott was crawling, Dort cooked, and Bob's younger sister, Linda, who had come along for the ride, agreed to babysit. I was happy to get a break from full-time motherhood and thankful to have others share the responsibility. Scott learned to walk on the three-plus-week boat trip, but this caused a problem. One of us needed to constantly watch him.

"Do you notice he sometimes walks with a list? "I asked my new in-laws.

"That's normal," Speed told me. "He's correcting himself to the movement of the water."

I wondered later if my son's calmly adapting himself on a moving boat resulted in his having become so centered all his life in his walk, his demeanor, and disposition. He had found his *sea legs*.

The winter in Florida arrived early in 1964, mirroring the entire Midwest. Not able to settle into what I thought would be warm walks on the shoreline and outside activities with my eleven-month-old son, I was instead in Dort's art class painting yellow bougainvillea.

"I don't believe there a*re* yellow bougainvillea," my mother-in-law told me. She had continued teaching her classes soon after we arrived. The other five students agreed with her. "No such thing, all my life, I never seen a yeller one."

That didn't matter to me. I fell in love with one small section I had painted. It was a perfect abstract rendition of a leaf, yet wasn't realistic enough for the accomplished "nothing but realism, exact copy of nature" art expert, Dort. She picked up her brush and before I could say, "No, not that one!" Dort added a stroke to my masterpiece, ruining the painting in my eyes. I did finish it *and* the four weekly sessions, though without ever again reaching that one masterful application. I never took another class from her and did not return to painting for twenty-five years.

We were safely docked on the neighbor's property in Avalon Beach. Scott was in a leash-like halter, tied to the railing. He loved having free rein and was always smiling, going in every direction possible. Speed and Linda promised to babysit while Dort and I were away.

When we returned from the painting class after a few hours, Scott was dangling by his harness, hanging over the edge of the boat. His feet were swishing around in the water as he sang to himself, "La, la, wawa, la la." I was horrified and angry at Speed and Linda for not watching him.

"I just checked on him a minute ago and he was on deck playing with his toys," Speed told me, as he pulled my son out of the bay. I unleashed Scott and took him below to our cabin, put on our bathing suits, grabbed a few towels and jackets, and hand-in-hand, we went along the shore, far from the boat. Even with the cold, it was time he learned to swim. It was also time to go back home.

The end of the school year in Florida couldn't come soon enough for me. Living on a fifty-two-foot boat with Bob and his family had been a great experience for a few months. I bonded with my in-laws and helped them achieve their dream of retirement to Florida, but by April, with its hot, humid days, I was eager to pack up a rental car. With Scott in tow, I drove to the college and waited in the parking lot for Bob to come out of his last class. After five months in Florida, I needed my friends and the familiarity of home.

Scott with his mom (author), c. 1964 – 1970,
PA and UNI

CHAPTER SIX

MINNEAPOLIS

We returned to Minneapolis in 1965 and rented a two-bedroom duplex a block from Nicollet Park.

When Scott was a baby, Bob and I reconnected with our high school friends in Minneapolis and were, again, happy to see them. *Dining Out* coupon books were a popular way for young couples to afford eating out at restaurants. One free meal for one paid allowed us to discover a new restaurant once a month. Bob and I, along with our best friends and other couples, were all newly married with babies. I got dressed up in a sleek colorful pantsuit and big hair, lots of makeup and jewelry, to go out drinking and eating.

One night, a friend from high school and I had a contest for how many brandy Manhattans we could consume. Steve, an athlete, was six foot three, weighed about 250, and was a very big drinker. I was five foot eight and weighed 125. We counted thirteen drinks each before we were both under the table. Steve had passed out and everyone there agreed I had won the bet. My worries about having a problem with alcohol disappeared as it turned out I was really good at it. Or so I thought.

My drinking had started when I was fourteen. I was at my best friend Heidi's confirmation party. As was customary, wine was offered to all by her German father. I drank several glasses and passed out, unaware that alcoholism was deeply embedded in me through Irish and Swedish ancestors.

Friday football games or hay rides were opportunities for Heidi or me to get an older person to buy the blackberry brandy or orange vodka we preferred. I have little memory of those events, just stories told to me by others. When I knew I was pregnant, my drinking decreased but was not totally absent. It would be another twenty years before warnings came out about pregnancy and alcohol. I wanted to believe that my children were unaffected at birth and, through denial, told myself that whatever damage alcoholism did to my children came much later, after they were born.

We lived less than half a block from a liquor store, and one day while Scott took his nap, I called in an order and ran over to get a bottle of brandy for a dinner party that evening. During my ten minutes away, the phone rang, waking Scott, age three. He had climbed out of his crib to answer the phone. Bob's grandmother, a devout Christian, asked her grandson, "Where's Mommy?"

"She's to the likker store." Scott said. I nervously laughed when hearing the story repeated but deep down was devastated. I always overexplained the incident, attempting to justify my behavior to all who heard the embarrassing account.

The following year, in June 1968, shortly before our daughter, Kim, was born, our family had grown to six. Dort, Speed, and Bob's sister, Linda, had moved into our second-story duplex apartment for the summer. They said it was "to help with the new baby," but I believed they wanted to escape the hot Florida weather. My workload was hardly improved and my stress level was high from anxiety about the soon-to-be birth and the extra chores—like cleaning out the bathtub for six and climbing two stories to do laundry every day after the doctor had said, "No stairs or bending."

Kim was also born early, on June 21st. She was a beautiful baby, but she had colic for the first three months and cried nightly until two or three in the morning. My mother-in-law, father-in-law, sister-in-law, and four-year-old Scott were no more than little help. Bob worked every day and needed to sleep, and I felt Scott needed my attention often in order to not become jealous of his baby sister. I was a nervous mess.

Speed was a daily drinker and usually wanted company for his afternoon "cocktail." Happily, I would often indulge, and by the time the three extended family members moved out several months later, I'd become more than a weekend drinker.

While continuing to take hundreds of pictures, I knew I needed more training in photography. There had been no decent art classes in high school and the instructions my brother Tom had given me were mostly "technical." I signed up for the Famous Photographers' Correspondence Course in Westport, Connecticut, with Phillipe Halsman, Richard Avedon, Irving Penn, and others—but learning photography from books and the delay receiving corrected lessons became unsatisfactory. Years later, when my kids were both in school, I enrolled in photography and drawing classes at the local college, happy to be making photograms, drawings, and collage. I began to identify myself as an artist.

In 1969, after six years of renting apartments Bob and I decided to buy our own place. Scott was five and Kim was one. I searched ads, looking only for properties under the $24,000 price we could afford. I thought a bigger house and better location would correct my growing discontent. On a beautiful spring day, I met my friend Heidi at a duplex for sale on Harriet Avenue in South Minneapolis. While we waited for the real estate agent to get there, we walked a few houses up the street to a large white house with a FOR SALE BY OWNER sign. In the back yard, apple trees were in bloom, and I imagined myself in the garden, digging in tulip bulbs and potatoes. I could feel the soft cushion on the lounge chair while sitting in the sun, watching my children play. I would plan my birthday party on the back porch, imagining it would be a surprise.

In this house there would be no fighting, as there had been before in the living room, no boredom or crying many nights in the bedroom, and no anger or loneliness in the kitchen—all of which I experienced earlier when beginning to feel I had picked the wrong man and married too young. Continuing to lay in the bed I had made, at least we would be in a new space. It was a magical house, four stories including an attic and basement with hauntings from spirits the kids and I befriended during our ten years there.

When I asked Scott to pick out the color of paint he wanted for his bedroom, he chose royal blue and played in his sun-filled room for hours under the window looking over the backyard. His box of toys held games and action figures, science projects, microscope and telescope—all mastered in little time.

At seven years old, Scott was spending hours in the basement. I stored boxes of blankets, clothes, wigs, etc. close to the washing machine and sink downstairs. The next morning, I saw that Scott had created a dressing room. The blanketed area would house costumes, wigs, and makeup required for productions he planned. I often wondered if Scott's later need for long periods of privacy came from those episodes.

In school, Scott would do a ten-page report instead of the required two pages. School, though, was not enough for him, and every chance he had—with neighbor friends, his sister, or cousins helping—he would stage a play or film, using parts of the house or other locations nearby.

During the first five years at home, I parented, cooked, sewed drapes, made covers for furniture, and cleaned out junk drawers several times a week while Bob went to work every day. I felt a growing need for more stimulation. Scott and Kim were both in school, so I took a part-time job with Polaroid, introducing the SX camera to buyers and dealers in Minnesota and South Dakota. I also worked for a company of sales representatives for Remington products. I hired the sales staff to sell Hot Combs, electric combs that blew hot air, in stores around the Twin Cities.

Making extra money for new clothes I desired for the kids or myself or having shag carpeting installed wasn't enough. I wanted to further my dream of studying photography and needed more than the correspondence course I had taken when Scott was a baby. In 1974 I enrolled at Metropolitan Community College for an AA degree and signed up for art and photography classes. I paid my own tuition and created a studio and darkroom in the basement, next to Scott's dress-up room. I began to photograph nature, family, and friends while drawing and collaging.

I also started to drink several nights during the week, after the kids went to bed, while Bob was working in the garage on his car, motorcycle, or boat.

Scott's curiosity and creativity had been apparent from an early age. He was always the ring leader—orchestrating, producing, and directing plays and 8mm films. He entertained us while making his characters become more beautiful. His four-and-a-half-years younger sister, Kim; cousins; neighbors; and friends—along with whomever else he could corral—would be dressed by Scott in old clothes from my mother's and my attics. With his ability to excite others and achieve the "look" he wanted, new identities emerged—and through poise and style, his child actors became more graceful versions of themselves, or of Scott's imagination.

After completing a Women's Studies class in college, my newfound knowledge of the other half through *her story* awakened countless needs for myself and my kids. I found new ways to raise Kim, giving her a fair chance to grow up *equal*, as I realized that Scott and Bob had privileges granted them due to my upbringing in patriarchy. I had Scott help in the kitchen while asking Kim to take out the garbage.

Scott in my blue prom dress with cousin
Karen. c. 1971 -1973, PA

CHAPTER SEVEN

ENTREPRENEURSHIP

When Scott was seven, our five-year-old next-door neighbor came to the door with his mother. He was crying. Billy idolized Scott and followed him everywhere, as did most of his cousins and the neighbor's kids. Whatever Scott told Billy to do, he did—chores or dares—without flinching. I noticed that Billy's hand was held tightly in his angry mother's grip.

"Your son took money from Billy for this stupid rock," she said.

"Let me see." I took the tin foil covered rock from her hand, and while turning it several times said, "Oh, this is one of his better ones. How much did he charge Billy?"

Scott had a large collection of rocks from many excursions to nearby lakes and rivers and discovered if he put foil around an interestingly shaped rock, it could be "art" and therefore saleable. This was long before the "pet rock" came on the market.

"A quarter, and I'm *sure* you won't mind returning the money." Billy's mother was a Republican who argued with me over Nixon's economic policies. Now she seemed very upset at what I thought of as my son's simply smart marketing of his art. *Other* adults had just smiled or laughed.

I called Scott, who came in dressed in a cape and makeup. He was preparing a play for his sister's birthday party later that day. "What's wrong?" he asked Billy, who went running to Scott, putting his arms around him. I explained that it was up to him whether or not he should return the money.

"It's okay. This is one of my best rocks, from Wisconsin, worth a dollar, but I'll give you your money back." Scott gave Billy a quarter, then whispered something in his ear, and a smile replaced the crying.

"Sorry," Scott said to Billy's mother.

Later, when the family came for the party, all the cousins went downstairs to Scott's dressing room. He had written a play about a princess in distress, and there were roles for all of the kids. From his vast wardrobe, he dressed each of them as a character for the play.

"Pleeeazzzz, Mom?" he would ask with an endearing smile when he wanted to use a special dress or wig. I no longer had use for my dress-up clothes, prom dresses, or wigs from the sixties, so he got most of what he asked for. Who could resist the impish look on his face or his passion for directing others. He brought out their best quality for each play through his generosity and creative, carefree yet serious, determination.

When Scott came up from the basement to give me the signal that I was to seat all the adults, the doorbell rang, and there stood Billy and his mother. *Uh-oh, now what?*

"Billy said Scott invited him to be in the play this afternoon," she sheepishly stated.

"Of course," I invited her to stay and watch and sent Billy downstairs.

When I finished seating everyone, little Billy came in wearing a black cape and dark makeup. He was carrying a large silver tray filled with aluminum foil covered rocks surrounding the inside of a basket.

"Twenty-five cents each," he said, as he offered them to all the adults. They laughed or smiled, some pulled out pockets, wallets, or purses. I was unsure of the money aspect but *more* uncertain how the audience would accept my son, dressed as a princess, the star of the play. I suspected he could be gay and wondered if others did.

ENTREPRENEURSHIP

At the end of the play, Billy ran up to Scott with a full basket of money.

"Who put the dollar bills in?" Scott asked.

"My mom bought three and paid a dollar for each, then others paid a dollar," Billy smiled.

Scott was smart about money, unusual for a child, but in a family struggling to buy any extras, he caught on fast.

A few years later, Bob came home from work on a summer day and saw Kim, our five-year-old daughter, pushing the lawn mower in the front yard. Her arms were over her head in order to reach the handle.

"Why are *you* mowing? That's Scott's job," he asked her. We had negotiated with Scott to mow the lawn for $5 a week.

"Scott's paying me $3 a week to mow." Kim said. We looked at each other and smiled but couldn't get mad at either of them.

Scott had movie nights for the neighbor kids where he showed his latest production along with a Laurel & Hardy or Charlie Chaplin 8mm film. He charged ten cents—and his sister, five cents—admission. One evening when I was cleaning up after dinner, Kim came running into the kitchen.

"Scott wants me to pay to see the movie. Why do *I* have to pay? It's *my* house too." I gave her a nickel.

For several years, my son had a coin collection. When friends, neighbors, or family came for a party at our house, Scott would ask each one of the adults if they had any rare coins. When they pulled some out from pocket or purse, Scott looked carefully at each coin and usually picked one or two, asking if he could add them to his "collection." I approved of his entrepreneurship and started looking closer at my coins.

In fifth grade, Scott had an assignment to write a story on something he loved. He chose money as the subject. A half century later, I still have the ten-page report he did, pictures and all. I think he sold it to me for $25.

Kim and Scott, c. 1970, PA

CHAPTER EIGHT

EXPANDING

I was digging in the garden one late-spring day when my sweet little boy asked, "What is your favorite flower?" Scott was probably six or seven.

I sat up on my heels, thinking. "Irises," I said, looking at the patch by the garage.

"Why do you like them?" he asked.

"Because they remind me of orchids, with their interesting shapes, elegant uniqueness and beauty. And they grow outside without much care." I explained the expense and rarity of orchids, how they don't grow in our climate and why we didn't have them in the house with the many indoor plants, where a toddler or cat could wreck them.

"Orchids are delicate and when knocked over, they could die. When Kim gets a bit older, we'll buy one." I told him.

Scott asked if he could pick some irises.

"Yes, but don't expect them to last more than a day in water."

The following year Scott bought me an orchid for my birthday. We put it up high, on a bookcase, on the back porch, in the sun. His love for orchids lasted his entire life, as did his love for astronomy.

Scott enjoyed looking at stars long before his first telescope at age seven. The sky at night was his navigational course as he entered an unknown, unexplored world. He seemed to study the universe as one studies the mind, looking into expanses of mystery to find vast, hidden truths. The lure of the cosmos intrigued him all his life. While I read science fiction, Scott looked through the telescope fantasizing another planet, a different existence.

All his life, the stars and sky fascinated my son. He bought at least seven telescopes and a computer that controlled the larger telescope he had set up outside. It revealed the planets, moon, and stars to him while he was inside, when it was too cold to be out, even when wearing the thermal silk underwear and battery-powered socks I had given him as requested Christmas or birthday presents.

"Look . . ." he would lure me to the screen or eye piece to see a solar flare or eclipse. Scott, excited, seemed to become an alien from another planet, searching for his real home. As he focused on the sky, I imagined he was tapping into modifying his own reality while taking me to new heights.

I remembered the day he gave me a meteorite, a prized heavy piece of metal from another galaxy, another time zone. It was as if it came from where *he* may have come from, a million years ago. It reminded me that we are all universal and have continuity, a past.

* * *

My brother Tom's wife, Jan, told me that when she babysat Scott, he was always the Quiet One. His facial expressions rarely changed. Always in deep thought, he took in and studied all that was around him.

"While his cousins were busy playing baseball, ice skating, or participating in other sports, Scott usually was calmly standing by the side," Jan said.

"He had no interest in sports but was probably anticipating his next adventure or production," I told her, knowing he would brilliantly orchestrate another play or film, an early indicator of his future career.

When he was ten, Scott announced he was going to learn German.

"How does any kid, on his own, decide to learn German?" Aunt Jan asked. I believed it was because of his German godmother, Heidi, my best friend from age eleven, who encouraged him.

Jan also admired his musical ability, amazed at how he mastered the piano. When Scott was eight years old, my neighbor was selling an upright piano, and we bought it from her, moved it across the street to our house on Harriet Avenue, and put it in our vestibule. Several hours later, I heard Scott Joplin music playing over and over and believed it to be the record we owned.

"Scott, please turn off that record!" I shouted from the kitchen. "You've been playing it over and over for an hour."

After an immediate silence Scott answered, "That was *me* playing."

I was astounded. He had taught himself the song simply from listening to the record. Scott always had a good ear for music, and piano lessons began soon after the Joplin incident. With his long fingers, deep level of comprehension and alert detachment, he seemed to transform the keys into an experience of escape and inventiveness. He celebrated, explored, and got lost in the music. Playing the piano became a daily study for Scott well into his late teens and beyond.

To *me*, at times, it sounded as though he was visiting another world—a happy one, where angels surrounded him as he played a Chopin ballad or Mozart sonata. He continued to play Bach, Mozart, Beethoven, Chopin, Debussy—and of course, Joplin—with enthusiasm, concentrated engagement, and serious purpose for the rest of his life.

Scott, c. 1968-1970, PA

CHAPTER NINE

FINDING IDENTITY

Scott's inspiration was often derived from TV and magazines. As Ziggy Stardust, David Bowie personified a transgender character in the early seventies through makeup and women's clothing. My son became fascinated by his otherworldly persona and his ever-changing sexual orientation. Bowie identified himself as first bisexual, then gay, then straight with wife and kids, while he explored the depth of what it meant to be a rock star.

Still gathering the neighborhood kids, his sister, and cousins to perform in plays, films, and shows, Scott was coming into his own identity at the age of eight. The kids became his canvas, and doing their makeup was a finishing touch. Scott usually took the starring female role.

Photographs show his creativity in glam and fashion, but what they don't show is what I believed was a recognition and celebration of women through his ability to transform whomever and whatever he envisioned. Often, the musicals and plays were performed in our living room in front of an audience of embarrassed and sometimes shocked adults. Boys who dressed in girls' clothes were not well accepted in the early seventies, and there were fixed social rules in the Midwest. Any sexuality other than hetero was taboo.

While slipping away from the "norm" made one untrustworthy, I dreaded I would be ostracized on so many levels by allowing my son to dress as a female *and* by my being an artist who photographed nudes. Men and women are all born from, and with, both x and y chromosomes. We all have male and female genes that at times could swing from one end of the spectrum to the other. Gender was my preferred photographic subject matter and was also often included as a key theme in Scott's favorite performances. Fear of being repudiated did not stop us.

The poet Rene Ricard wrote, "Every minute somewhere in the world parents are finding children in drag." I loved the shows and was always proud of Scott, even if surprised at times for feeling somewhat awkward or flustered. It was complicated. I was a feminist and my son's dressing as a woman seemed like flattery, complementing and honoring the female, celebrating feminine flair. In that era of excess and sexual experimentation, Scott, like David Bowie, explored opportunities that the alienated young could look up to as a pathway to uniqueness. Androgyny and ambiguity, if not acceptable, were certainly no longer strange.

Bowie's boldness and innovation delivered magic to Scott and others identifying themselves as something other than the norm. He was taking elements from different areas that didn't fit with each other. Bowie and Scott would try one thing, then another, a stepping stone to the next alternate world. The outlying things were pushed together, comprising surprise and delight in a bag of colorful performances. "Turn and face the strange." Bowie said.

FINDING IDENTITY

Scott with cousin Mark, c. 1974 - 1980,
PA and UNI

Heidi's daughters Lisa and Tanya with Scott
(as Simon Legree) and Kim in Omaha, c. 1974,
PA

CHAPTER TEN

PRODUCTIONS AND PERFORMANCES

The arguing between Bob and I grew more intense, and after a year of unhelpful marriage counseling and another year of my seeing a divorce counselor, Bob moved out of the house a month before Scott's eleventh birthday. I had gone through the separation from their father in 1974, when I was twenty-nine; Scott, ten; and Kim, six. It was liberating for us. Scott had no desire for sports or cars, and his father had no interest in theater, makeup, fashion, or art. After Bob left the house, I was less strict with my son and never interfered with his artistic output. At that time, he was making films and was spending part of a summer vacation with Kim at his godmother Heidi's house in Omaha, Nebraska.

He took with him one of his most prized possessions. Not Ben, his pet rat that I reluctantly agreed to care for–but an 8mm movie camera, which he had recently received as a present.

Heidi later said, "Anyone who knew Scott would tell you he loved to entertain and bring fantasy, excitement, and joy into others' lives." The day she remembered so vividly was the day he and Kim, along with Heidi's daughters, Lisa and Tanja, set out to make a movie. It was to feature Simon Legree and three damsels in distress. Simon Legree was the villain from Harriet Beecher Stowe's *Uncle Tom's Cabin*. Scott was not only the director, photographer, costume designer, makeup artist, and stunt man, but also the star of the movie, Simon.

On the day of the shoot, the kids went with their lunch into the Prairie Lane neighborhood to find a good location for filming. Those were days we let the kids roam free, but by mid-afternoon Heidi had not seen any sign of them. She became concerned and went to hunt them down. They lived near the Union Pacific railway line, and as she climbed a hill approaching the railroad, Heidi saw, to her horror, her two precious daughters and Kim tied with dainty pink ribbons to the Union Pacific tracks. Scott, with his mustache, was rolling the camera. Not knowing the train schedule, Heidi panicked, rescued the damsels in distress, and according to Scott, ruined the film. She later wrote, "a memory of a gentle soul, who wasn't so gentle the day I recall." The days of letting our kids roam free without fear ended soon after that incident.

Earlier that year I had enrolled at Metropolitan Community College, and students working in photography had the opportunity to join the school's video club. Allowed to take home equipment on the weekends, I checked out the Portapak, a half-inch videotape machine.

"I thought I would tape your play tonight." It was more of a question than a statement. Scott, especially excited, with a glowing face, agreed, and went straight down to his dressing room in the basement. Usually, he dressed the neighbor kids and his sister first but this time I didn't see him until suppertime, a few hours later, and only one hour before guests were to arrive for my mother's sixty-ninth birthday celebration. I suspected he was gathering a special outfit and making changes in the play script, as he'd planned to be featured in the production himself. After eating only a few bites, he went back down to the dressing room.

There were thirteen kids and nine adults, including my mother, sister, two brothers, and their spouses and children who all got together several times a month for holidays, birthdays, someone's pay raise, a child winning an award, or other occasions. This was a special night and neighbors were also invited. Even Scott's father was there, though we had recently separated. Some of the cousins opted out of the play as they thought it "kid stuff." Others thought maybe it would be a bit "raunchy" for them. But most, Scott's age and younger, were eager performers.

One by one, the kids came to the door with big eyes, asking Scott, their *director*, "What am I wearing?" Within a half hour, each came up dressed in outrageous combinations of colorful slinky sequined dresses, skirts, or tops—some pinned to fit. The feather boas made me think it would be a twenties review. The music Scott had on the turntable was Scott Joplin ragtime.

The adults made drinks and ate chips and nuts and settled into seats in the large living room as the actors, with disorder and flurry, took their places. Scott arrived last, looking like a young famous actress or ten-year-old musical performer dressed in sparkling, see-through thigh-high tights and miniskirt with a tassel hip belt and tube top. He wore several boas, black gloves, sunglasses, a blond wig, and had painted ruby-red lips. Scott walked the part of a movie star or street tart, holding a cigarette. This dramatic personality was new to me. I wondered if he was dressing for the video or the larger audience. While a bit embarrassed, I was proud and delighted by my son's odd talent. His father however, shrunk with his head down, visibly ashamed.

"This is too much," Bob said, loud enough for many to hear.

"I hope there's nothing in this play in bad taste," he whispered to me, looking at Scott, who looked at me. I was humiliated, both for Bob's discomfort and Scott's new identity as a sex tart. It helped that I'd had several drinks by then and saw my mother smiling and laughing nervously. I had increased my drinking after Bob moved out, thinking—*now no one will accuse me of having a problem.* Scott was oblivious to any embarrassment, negativity, or doubt.

Videotape was expensive and the school would not let us keep the recorded reel after we rented the machine. I knew others would record over it unless there was a taped note: DO NOT RECORD OVER. I wanted a chance to make a copy and put notes on the tape, the Portapak machine, the camera, and the case—yet somehow they went unread or ignored. When I checked the tape a few days later, it had been recorded over with my classmate's brother's football game. But Scott was not upset that his production was lost forever. He had found his calling.

The next day, Scott asked if he could "borrow" any old clothes of mine with fringe, sparkles, or sequins that I no longer wore.

"I'm planning Act II and have ideas for more dancers," he said as I smiled, happy to see he was encouraged by most of the audience, especially his mother and grandmother. We searched my closet and the sewing room together as I wondered again, with ambivalence, if he was gay.

Scott, c. 1974, PA

CHAPTER ELEVEN

FLO AND FREEDOM

I met Florynce Kennedy in the first year at college in 1974, when my sociology professor asked if I wanted to cohost Flo during a radio and lecture tour in Minneapolis. He had written a book about her and knew I would be tough enough to handle an outspoken feminist for a few days. *People Magazine* called her "the biggest, loudest and, indisputably, the rudest mouth on the battleground where feminist activists and radical politics join...."

"Come in, the door's unlocked," I heard when I knocked at her room in the Lemington Hotel. She was reclining on the bed wearing a leather cowboy hat, leather vest, and skintight pants. She had on pink sunglasses that partially hid her false eyelashes. I was surprised to see those as well as her bright-red lacquered fingernails and ruby-red lipstick. I thought a feminist would have no such embellishments.

"I've lost three feet of intestines and my spine is fused together by God knows what. I shouldn't be alive but here I am, too outrageous and stubborn to die."

I laughed. Flo ordered me to sit on the bed and I did. She moved a bit to one side, but I was afraid of her, and she knew it.

"Honey, don't be afraid of me or anyone—ever!" She put on her riding boots.

"Don't agonize–*organize!* Now let's get going." We were out the door minutes later.

Flo Kennedy had applied and been rejected by Columbia

Law School in the late forties, told it wasn't due to her color, but the fact that she was a woman. Flo threatened a law suit and was admitted, graduating in 1951, preceding Ruth Bader Ginsburg. She represented Billie Holiday and Charlie Parker, who both taught her that the law was not an effective means of changing society. Flo turned to political activism and sued the Catholic Church and many corporations, including Standard Oil. She founded the Feminist Party in 1971 and led numerous boycotts and protests, many of which I joined. Her lecture tour with Gloria Steinem was described by Gloria as "the Thelma and Louise of the seventies."

"I had to speak first because after Flo, I would have been an anticlimax." Gloria said. While onstage, a disgruntled man asked Flo if she and Steinem were lesbians.

"Are you the alternative?" Flo asked. I was reminded of Dorothy Parker's words, "Heterosexuality is not normal, it's just common."

Flo had dabbled in acting and was comfortable onstage. I was not. After her rousing speech against the Vietnam War, sexism, racism, oppression, and political apathy at the University of Minnesota, Flo called me up onstage to sing "We shall Overcome." We held our fists high above our heads. Scott admired her outfits and audacity, and she loved the idea of him dressing up in women's clothes and performing. In New York years later, they formed a friendship.

* * *

I became radicalized while my progressive disease of alcoholism fast forwarded through the seventies and took on another mutation. I started dating a college schoolmate. Craig was tall, black, and truly beautiful. We met through the college's video club and were immediately enamored with each other. No one had ever shown that much passionate love and respect for me, and we became a couple until my third year in college. He loved my kids but also liked to drink, and with him, I began an addiction to love and sex along with alcohol.

In 1975, Craig gave me a book, *Discover Yourself through Photography*, and a blank journal, encouraging me to make art and write down my ideas and thoughts. We stayed friends after he left for LA to attend film school, and I began dating others while at the College of Art and Design, studying photography, video, and collage.

I drew sketches in early pages of the journal. One of the drawings has me sitting in an arm chair I had reupholstered during my stay-at-home years. Scott is on my right side and Kim on the left. It was for a photo, but when I developed the photographs, the arm chair was empty—only the kids were at each side. It was supposed to be a family portrait but I had pressed the wrong button and the self-timer didn't work. This photo spoke to me years later, depicting my psychological separation from the kids due to my growing addictions. I had gone missing.

I had another idea—to video a woman's face (representing me) with her hands pulling in the sides of the frame to close in on her/me as the camera zoomed in. I felt locked inside a box.

During the summers, Scott and Kim would spend several months with their father, and I used the time to make art and write. The first weeks were always lonely until the time to myself felt like freedom. I opened up to unlimited possibilities. That same year, I started to smoke marijuana when my children were in school. I only dated men who liked to drink and smoke pot and told myself love, sex, and drugs were important for art. By the fall of 1976, I wrote in my journal: *I'm going to try to give up men again. They tire me out and take all my energies ... I can't seem to get back to myself and have fleeting moments of uncertainty ... There's such an emptiness inside ... I can't listen to love songs or watch certain movies on TV for fear I'll break down and cry again.*

Me and Scott, c. 1974, UNI

CHAPTER TWELVE

SEX EDUCATION

I can't recall when I realized my son was no longer a part of me, when I no longer needed to fill his days with fun and creative tasks or answer his questions. But soon it was clear he began to question my answers.

When I was a girl of twelve, I was with a friend making small books of art and stories for an imagined class I would be teaching in a school. Later, grown up in the mid-seventies, I still had the same dream of teaching art or photography at a college somewhere. Until then, I believed my kids were my students, my understudies who relied and depended on my guidance. They were an extension of me.

I felt ready for the "sex" talk when the boys came into the living room.

"Mom, where do babies come from?" my son asked me after school one day. He was with his neighborhood friend, Brad—thirteen, a year older than Scott. They approached me as I was reading a textbook on video production.

I remembered my own introduction to sex. A neighborhood friend, Patty, who was thirteen, told me when a boy put his penis into the girl's belly button, he injected a seed that grew into a baby. I believed her. After all, she was a year older than I was and knew many things I didn't know. That summer, to be safe, I put away all my short tops in the back of the dresser and spent the next several months carefully covering my belly button.

Certainly, I didn't want my children to hear this sort of nonsense, so sixteen years later, on another soon-to-be summer day, I was ready. Janis Ian's "At Seventeen" was on the radio. She sang about dancing, dreaming, and obscenities.

I asked Scott and Brad to sit down and explained to them, as best I could, the exact clinical description of a man and woman making a baby, information I had gleaned from either the seventh- or eighth-grade gym class, a family health course in college, and life experience. Both boys seemed calm and interested while I sweated through the lecture. Towards the end of it, my son interrupted.

"Naw, that doesn't sound right to me. Come on, Brad, let's go play outside." They turned away as Scott said, "Thanks anyway, Mom."

"Well, wait a minute, I ..." and they were out the door. Relieved that I didn't have to continue, I returned to my book. It was the seventies, sex was everywhere, but I didn't want to bring up the subject again. I had done my duty. It was not my fault if he didn't believe me. Also, if he was gay, he may not have wanted or cared to know. I wasn't prepared to have the "gay discussion" yet. I kept quiet.

That night, we watched our favorite comedian, Jonathan Winters, on TV in a skit where he was kicking a head of cabbage around. I started laughing uncontrollably. Winters, with squinty eyes and forced smile, had answered an interviewer's question about why he was kicking a cabbage.

"Mother told me so," he answered seriously. I doubled over on the two-tone, olive-green shag carpeting, not able to stop my bizarre rollicking laughter over the puzzling link between a mother and cabbage. Tears began running down my face.

Scott first looked at me with a smile then joined in the fun, tumbling unto the floor, holding his stomach from his aching side-splitting laughter. The absurdity of Jonathan Winters' outlandish and eccentric humor connected to my earlier explanation of sex in a way I cannot explain, but it left a long, impossible-to-replicate memory of bonding with my son, a moment now precious to me.

"The one thing about art I like, and I still do: You're in charge," Jonathan Winters had said.

Years later, I searched for hours online through videos of Jonathan Winters' work but I never found the cabbage routine. Like my time with Scott, it was as if it had been a dream.

Scott with my Retina IIIC camera, c. 1974, PA

Drawing of me (by me) on Photo with Scott and Kim, c. 1976, PA

CHAPTER THIRTEEN

GRADUATE SCHOOL AND JERRY GARCIA

I was irritable, yelling at the kids, frustrated, depressed, and uninspired about everything. Something had to change. I was losing my family. Instead of giving love and attention to my kids, I had been trying to fill an empty void and became addicted to any drink, drug, or man I met. Alcohol continued to be my favorite. Luckily, heroin was never offered.

Linda Ronstadt sang about how easy it is to fall in love as I searched for the right man. Every few months, I had a new boyfriend or two and wondered later what must it have been like for Scott, becoming a man, or Kim, seeing their mother drinking and having so many boyfriends? I wanted love and happiness but what I felt was indifference.

"What happened to Jay?" Scott asked one day before Gary was coming over for dinner.

"I'm not seeing him anymore," I answered, stirring pasta sauce on the stove.

"Why?" Scott put his finger in the sauce to taste it.

"He's got too many girlfriends," I explained. A few weeks went by and I was dating Reed.

"Where's Gary?" Scott asked.

"He's still around, we're just friends." After several similar moments of confusion, Scott stopped asking about any man who came over.

In April 1977, I was accepted at the University of Minnesota graduate school of Art and had much to be thankful for, yet something was lacking. I needed a close look at myself to find out why I was not more careful in picking boyfriends or was so quick to fall in love. I asked myself in my journal after each breakup, usually instigated by me: *Am I getting into relationships just to forget or cover up the pain from the past relationship?*

My friends were right in saying there was something in me causing this syndrome, the men I picked, and everything that followed. I was convinced the next relationship would go very slow, romantic that I was, but I needed a fantasy in order to be happy—one with unconditional love, no arguing, verbal abuse, or criticism. Something was missing from inside myself, and I had a fear I could not explain. I kept procrastinating, drinking, and getting high on pot most nights instead of doing household chores, helping my kids with homework, or making art. Scott, thirteen, kept busy with his productions, filming, and schoolwork while asking me, "Why are you always angry with everyone?"

One weekend I had a sick stomach, writing: *Gastritis or gall bladder will hopefully change my habits—no more excessive drinking ... How curious that things repeat themselves ... Quit putting such emphasis on relationships of intense nature ... Infatuation should be treated for what it is & no more ... I fall in love too quickly & too easily—slow down—concentrate more on work.*"

By July, each of my boyfriends was taking up too much of my time. All together, they were draining me. I wasn't working and wanted to be free and independent of men. I wanted to have my cake, eat it, and nibble on it too.

In August, I wrote: *Went to health clinic—I'm on a ten-day diet—no smoking, drinking, etc. —how horrid—I slept most of the day but got high later with Carter—I can't let this restrictiveness get me down—it's only for the best, anyway.*

I met Robert Carter—*yes, another Bob, though I called him*

"*Carter*"—at a party that summer and, by the time I found out he was a cocaine dealer, I was totally infatuated with him—or was it the cocaine? A new drug added to my list of addictive substances, plus a tall, handsome, loving man.

My mother watched the kids for the weekend while I went to a Grateful Dead concert with Carter, who enticed me to try my first LSD. Even with just a one-third hit, it sent me to a place far beyond this universe. I remember sitting at the top of the bleachers at the Civic Center in St. Paul, Minnesota, watching the multi-colored steps floating up and down as I received answers to all the questions everybody'd ever had throughout history. By the time Carter found me, I had forgotten all my new-found information. Lucky for me the forgetfulness and feeling out of control assured me of never becoming attached to LSD. I was too confused.

When I'd met Carter and found out he was a "deadhead," I had to ask what that meant. Other than Simon and Garfunkel and Sonny and Cher in the sixties, I had not latched on to any style or musical group. Dinners and parties at Carter's place always had Grateful Dead music, cocaine, and pot—and I usually went home high. Though we stopped dating after that first Dead concert because he fell in love with another woman, we continued to be friends.

I was in graduate school with all male professors, doing art they had never imagined or seen before and felt extreme pressure, having a ton of work to do over the weekend. But on a Friday morning, Carter called and asked if I wanted to go to the Dead concert in Wisconsin with him, his new girlfriend, and another male friend. The weekend he described would be a repeat of those fond memories from a time I wished to bring back. I called my mother and asked her to stay with Scott and Kim for the weekend.

The precognitive dream I had recorded in my journal on February 2, 1978 seemed clairvoyant:

I was at a family party and met a thin Santa Claus. He said,

"God, I don't believe it—how beautiful you are." His hair was unkempt, black, and wavy, with salt and pepper streaks throughout. Later in the dream, I could hear his phone ringing and went to the next room to try and listen to what he was saying.

At the concert in Madison, I watched Carter put his arm around his new girlfriend. They were a few feet ahead of me and, knowing they would move up towards the stage, I went to the front of the crowd. I wanted to divert my jealousy and avoid seeing them again. My eyes caught Jerry Garcia's eyes, fifty feet away on stage right. We locked sight and, while I moved to the left, he followed on stage right. It seemed as if he knew me and was playing the song, "Eyes of the World" or "Brown Eyed Woman" to me alone. I was enthralled.

Back at the hotel, where we all were staying, the phone in my room rang. Carter said, "Jerry's down here at the bar." He later claimed I got off the elevator before he hung up the phone, so eager was I to meet this telepathic "Santa Claus."

I went straight over to Jerry and said, "Hi, I'm Pat Horner."

One of the band members gave me his seat next to Jerry and that started a three-day fantasy. Garcia had studied art before becoming a musician and was very interested in my photography, video, and film work. We spoke for hours on what each of us liked, then spent the night together.

Having too much cocaine caused us to be fully awake, vibrant, and energetic at 4:00 a.m.

"I'm going swimming, want to come?" I asked.

"I don't do sports but I'll keep you company," Jerry answered. We had the pool to ourselves and I did laps to burn off the energy from the past several days while Jerry, in his usual black T-shirt and brown corduroys, walked back and forth on the edge of the pool closest to me. We talked about the education of our kids. Jerry was a chatterbox on cocaine, and I was happy to be wearing off the drugs.

"Do you know how schools got started?" he asked.

"No, how?" I was huffing and puffing from lack of exercise and the physical strain of swimming. After five minutes on schools and education, Jerry switched to art and filmmaking. We were both working on film ideas and discussing them led from topics about cosmic energy, physics, and consciousness to why we were so attracted to each other. I thought he was a true beatnik or hippie, not anti-anything. Somehow, he was able to enter my wavelength, my psyche. I wondered if he was addicted to all the drugs he took.

Jerry was going to Iowa for the next two concerts and invited me. I called my mother to ask if she could spend another few days watching the kids. She happily agreed. We got to the airport, and there was a small Cessna plane the guys from the band had arranged so that Jerry and I could be alone together. The flight was short, beautifully sunny and smooth.

I woke the next day alone in bed at a motel in Cedar Falls, Iowa and saw Jerry drawing on the frosted window in our motel room. Rising quietly, I put on boots and grabbed my 8mm camera and coat. I started to film him, first from inside before going out the door to get his drawing on glass in better light. It must have been thirty below outside. He continued with the abstract design, filling up the entire window. When the film ran out, I went inside.

"You *are* a true artist!" I told him. He hugged me and smiled, pleased and proud.

On the airplane trip home a few days later, I decided to finish my last roll of 8mm film from my window seat, shooting the beautiful clear sky over pillow-like clouds. When I got the films developed, Scott and I watched both, although Scott preferred David Bowie. The Jerry drawing on window film was fine but there were circles and flashing lights throughout the airplane film that must have happened during processing. Or was it Jerry's energy from our cosmic connection that followed the airplane?

Scott was thrilled when hearing my stories and seeing the films.

"Cool! Did you get his autograph?" He asked, smiling.

"No, but he was very interested in your performances and wants to meet you and Kim."

The three days and nights together with Jerry were mystical, magical, and monumental. My journal from February 6, 1978 reads: *Met Jerry Garcia three nights ago and my life has changed—or rather transformed.* I had finally met my match.

I listened to his records for messages to help me through difficulties with graduate work at the University of Minnesota. I knew we would be together again soon, and when he called, asking me to meet him in Pittsburgh, he would pay my way.

"Pittsburgh? No thanks. I need to study," I said. It was becoming clear to me that I needed to set limits around him.

I thought of Jerry as an intelligent, graciously kind man who sought out unexplored territory in both his music and his relationships. Exquisite in his discourse, attitudes, and actions, he never said anything bad about anyone while I was with him. When I complained of others' improper or stupid deeds, he would tell me, "Don't let them get you down." He didn't want to be a "guru" and didn't understand why people followed him. The Deadhead phenomenon was developed from his goodness as a deep old soul with higher energy who had evidently forgiven mankind of its own faults. Marijuana also played a big role in his and his supporter's lives.

He had been making artwork from early childhood and studied painting at the San Francisco Art Institute as a teenager, speaking often on how art has the power to reach and teach those who are seeking something beyond themselves. He had found himself through music and drugs. Lots of drugs.

"We have this intuitive thing," he would say, when we both knew what the other was thinking or feeling. I had been single for over three years and believed I was learning to be a better person, better artist, and a more understanding mother. Jerry had been single for eleven years when we met. In the song "Ripple" he sang about each path being individual and how no one could follow.

2/25/78–Jerry called! We talked for almost an hour–he misses me too!! I'm ecstatic. He's going on tour and I may see him in California after Mar. 19. I should have invited him here or offered to go to Pittsburgh or Rochester–better not jump into this. We talked about ups and downs and loving surprises–I want to surprise him somehow... There is a feeling of communicating with Jerry on a time/space level I don't understand. Need to mellow– my psyche cannot take so much expansion. My life is too hectic. I must slow down, spend the weekend with the kids, rest up, think and read. I wish Jerry would call.

He called the next day and another trip was planned for Chicago in May. I prepared and packed while putting kids, art, and school in order, thinking how wonderful it is to travel.

My mother was delighted to spend another three days with Scott and Kim. She was good with them and they loved her, always happy to go to her house. I was lucky to have her nearby.

Jerry and I took a walk on a street outside the Uptown Theater before the concert in Chicago. He loved being with people, anyone really, but he wanted a break from the frenzy of having a bodyguard and constant adoring fans approaching him. A few passersby said, "Hi Jerry, see you tonight," or other greetings. One of them, a hippie or bum, approached him and followed us for a few blocks.

"Hey man, could you get me tickets to the gig tonight?"

Jerry looked through his pockets, "Sorry, I don't have any on me."

"How about some cash or drugs?" Again, empty pockets. The bum looked at Jerry's sneakers and asked for those. Jerry was about to take them off when I reached in my purse.

"I have some money," I said. Jerry would have given him his new sneakers or anything he had on him. As we walked away, he recounted the story of buying the sneakers with his friend and bodyguard from the Hell's Angels. We returned to the safety of the concert hall, going in the back door labeled: EMPLOYEES WITH PASSES ONLY. I was in love again and in denial of our dependence on drugs and alcohol.

Living in Marin County, the Grateful Dead was considered the most successful touring band in the US. They were followed by a mass of Deadheads, fans drawn to the music and the philosophy, much of it misunderstood as a "drug permissive" and "anything goes" idea. The real philosophy, at least from what Jerry told me at the time I knew him, was one of love, goodness, acceptance, and peaceful desire to live the hippie dream with each other in search of higher knowledge and joy. I was not a Deadhead but simply someone, fueled by drugs, who fell in love with a musician. Or was I falling in love with drugs?

Later, Jerry gave me the book *Communication with Higher Intelligence* by Timothy Leary, and my mind and ideas expanded rapidly. There seemed to be no limit to my dependency while my drinking and drug use increased.

The best thing for me would be to sell the house, pick up the kids, and head for North of San Francisco, I wrote in my journal at the end of May while high. I was high every night then.

Scott and I were excited about the growing relationship between Jerry and me, even the idea of moving to California. We overlooked his drug use as I told Scott and myself that Jerry would stop if I asked him to. This sounds like a crazy statement now, but I believed it at the time.

I became concerned about the long-distance relationship and my doing more drugs and alcohol. It was affecting Scott and Kim. The three of us were fighting more, and they were not doing chores or helping when asked. We had started family counseling the month before and soon I was advised to give up the idea of relying on Jerry as a partner.

"Garcia is a drug addict and will not stop using, he's unstable for you and the children. It could be he loves drugs more than people. Do you want this chaotic life?" the counselor asked.

I was in denial about Jerry and myself as drug addicts. Yes, I'd become dependent but still believed we were smart enough to quit anytime we wanted. I know now it was delusional thinking.

Jerry invited me to go to Egypt for the outdoor concerts in September, and I wanted to go but knew that his ex-girlfriend, Mountain Girl, would be there with her daughter Sunshine. The counselor's warnings, along with my conscience, haunted me. I told Jerry, "I'll try," and began making Sphinx and Pyramid drawings as I cut down on drugs and my drinking.

6/17/78—I dreamed of a corner house collapsing during a family picnic. We evacuated ... I'm surprised that my intent on not smoking, getting high, or drinking has gone astray ... Egyptian images in my dream while I listened to Jerry singing about a blind man saying, "Don't you see?"

By the end of June, I admitted to myself that I was addicted, yet all I wanted was Jerry. On July 3rd, I went to the St. Paul Civic Center concert, thinking he had arranged the three-day event to be closer to me and Minneapolis.

I was excited, and wrote, *Jerry told me of his months-long morphine trip ... I awoke next morning with him touching me ... Knowing my love for him will never be realized and that it's a lifetime thing.* I knew the relationship could never work yet was unable to break it off.

In September, I went to Egypt and attended the three nights of Dead concerts, held outside between the Great Pyramid and the Sphinx. On the last night, the band played "Dark Star" as the Sahara moon underwent a total eclipse. Invited to the after-party in a large tent in the desert, I rode alongside Jerry on a camel but did not sleep with him. Mountain Girl and Jerry's daughter were usually with him. They must have known of our relationship yet did not interfere.

I spent another three weeks in Egypt, photographing and

traveling to Alexandria with a woman I met at the concert. I found an Egyptian lover for three days, and bought many leather or carved gifts for friends and family: a hand tooled leather portfolio for Scott and galabia (kaftan) for Kim. Scott kept some letters I had sent him along with personal papers inside the portfolio case until his death.

The drugs became too much, and without saying a word, Jerry and I moved on with our lives. As friends, I no longer fantasized a real relationship, I had chosen my children over love for a man. Jerry and I kept in touch periodically as I went to concerts where there were backstage passes left for me at the ticket booth.

The last time I saw Jerry was at Madison Square Garden, in New York, in 1989. We sat together backstage between sets. He listened to my tales of my own and Scott's sobriety, before he told me he had also given up drugs and alcohol.

"Yeah, the guys leaned on me and insisted." He confessed, as he held a glass of wine in one hand and what appeared to be a joint in the other.

* * *

Shortly after moving into our house in Willow, I had a dream the day Jerry died. It was a hot summer day—Sunday, August 9, 1995. At 5:00 a.m. I awoke to what sounded like a doorbell ringing but there was no doorbell in the house. I observed Jerry floating up to the sky with three female angels. They were wearing capes—the women in white and his in black. Jerry had a sweet, content, loving smile on his face. He seemed to be silently communicating to me that he was fine, all was well.

As I drove to work later that morning, I picked up a hitchhiker. I had never done that before but he had long hair and we were in Woodstock. *How dangerous could he be?* I thought to myself. On the way into town, he told me he was bummed out.

"I just found out my guru died this morning."

"Who was that?" I asked.

"Jerry Garcia. Do you know who that is?"

I had to pull over to the side of the road, the brakes screeched as I leaned over the steering wheel, stunned and in shock. The hitchhiker was quiet for what seemed like several minutes.

"He died of a heart attack, in a treatment center. He'd just turned fifty-three, eight days ago. I guess his long, strange trip finally came to an end."

But I knew it was drugs that killed Jerry, causing the heart to give out. It was several minutes before I could tell the stranger about my dream and a bit of my story. I was grateful to be sober and drug-free and recommitted to stay that way.

The hitchhiker and I got together several times to grieve as we listened to tapes and watched DVDs of The Grateful Dead. An era had ended for me.

Scott in Pittsburgh, 1980, PA

CHAPTER FOURTEEN

PITTSBURGH

To earn the $2,000 I needed for the Egypt trip, I started a job in August 1978 designing and selling outdoor advertising. Gulf Development was a California company that offered the possibility of making $1,000 per week. The kids were with their father, and I only had three weeks before my trip, but I was determined to succeed. The first week was training with no pay. By the end of the third week, I had the money.

From day-one , I was in love with Cairo and the way of life there—noisy, crowded, energetic yet peaceful and calm, even in the chaos of crumbling infrastructure and crazy traffic. The people seemed familiar, loving, and mysterious. I romanticized living there without a man, raising my children in a city that would mother us all. When I returned home, I continued the job with Gulf Development in order to afford to take my kids back to Egypt. Scott was almost as excited as I was. No longer dressing up, his interests had moved on to piano and astronomy.

I was determined to leave Minneapolis after I saved enough money. Then, *of course*, within a few weeks I fell in love with my district manager, Rick. My kids, friends—and even my mother—all liked him too. But I was skeptical, searching my journals for advice from myself, I found mostly a middle-aged feminist out of control, filled with self-pity, and blaming others. On September 23rd I wrote, *But I love many—how can I narrow it to one—and that one may not be the one a year from now. Rick now, last year*

Jerry, before that Carter, Reid, Richman, Craig, and those in between. What and who next year? Expectations, restrictions, and obligations—those are the reasons for not getting married ... I hate routine ... I will be wealthy someday, but never wealthier than I am now. My children and friends are more important to me than anything. The love I have for them is worth more than fortune.

Rick and I both got promoted at Gulf and were assigned to Pittsburgh, where I became a District Manager. Rick would be my Regional Manager. In December, Scott turned fifteen. He was becoming a beautiful young man. We loved our home, yet we were *all* excited for the move.

I rented out the Harriet Avenue house to a family and prepared to move furniture, kids, and cat by car and large truck from Minneapolis to Pittsburgh. In Chicago, our cat, Panther, escaped from the car and Kim and Scott insisted we find him before leaving. After several hours waiting for the cat, who finally returned, we drove all night through Ohio.

In Pittsburgh, we rented a brownstone townhouse in Squirrel Hill. The kids loved their schools and the neighborhood. They made new friends, and I hired the top pianist from the local symphony to teach Scott classical piano. Rick paid for most of the household costs and was generous to all of us. We explored the city together while welcoming the milder climate.

1/6/79—Monty (our family counselor in Minneapolis) *was right in saying, "One never escapes their problems or hassles" ... But here they're not as frustrating ... the emotional distress goes but I feel a certain emptiness ... The kids are happy, we're all happy, so why am I worried?*

My art, though, was not advancing and when visiting galleries, I often heard, "We do *not* show pots or photography," and other similar refusals. I was doing fine-art photography and my intuition for years had been that New York City was the only place for an artist with ambition and children who were creative. My frustration, dissatisfaction, and drinking increased as I suspected I would need help. But I chose alcohol over counseling.

We had taken Rick's furniture to Pittsburgh and I had rented my furnished house in Minneapolis to a government worker with great references. But after she stopped paying rent for three months, I had her evicted. She moved out, taking everything of value—my antiques, Scott's Lionel train set, and so much more.

4/5/79—Back to Minneapolis to clean house. There's a blizzard here, four birds sitting on the lilac tree, not much protection from the wind & snow. A beautiful blue & white-headed, grey-topped, fat-bellied bird sits in the fallen limb from the apple tree … I wonder why people live here. I wonder how birds got fat. I miss Pittsburgh, Rick, and the kids.

After cleaning the house, I rented it again—this time to a trusted friend. I filed a law suit against the government worker and arranged for my brothers to be managers. They would keep an eye on the house. I returned to Pittsburgh and my new life of motherhood and art.

"I feel like we are just slaves to you," Scott told me at our weekly family meeting, where the four of us aired requests and complaints. We had been in Pittsburgh five months. I was working three-days-a-week hiring and training a sales force for Gulf and trying to do art. My partner, Rick, was doing his best to play the loving main provider, parent, and partner—tasks he wasn't up for.

"I give you both chores that should take only twenty minutes or half an hour to do for three or five dollars a week. How is that slavery?" I asked.

"But we have homework and want to watch TV, like you do sometimes." Scott said, adding, "You're mean."

"I'm sorry you see me as mean," I answered, looking at both of my children.

"I'll try not to be." We all seemed satisfied, and I went to make myself a drink. I later wrote, *I'm realizing how much I'm addicted to drugs, and yet it's such a nice feeling.*

Mother's Day was coming up and I vowed to be as nice and attentive to them as I could possibly be—maybe take them to an art museum.

6/6/79—Finished reading Zelda. *Feeling depressed and fretful about how quickly life comes to such tragic endings ... Why do we mistreat the only vessel we have for such few pleasures that smoking and drinking give us? For the life of me, I cannot understand ... I can't get out of Pittsburgh soon enough ... We must leave this destructive city and self-destructive way of life. Rick and I are becoming F. Scott & Zelda—destroying ourselves as well as each other.*

Searching my journals for clues as to why I wasn't a better mother to my children proved depressing. My writings revealed an obsessive focus on my own art and my own inner, private life of sex and longing. I should have gone to therapy but believed I could handle my job, relationship, motherhood, new home, and art alone, by myself. There were times I took the kids out for ice cream, walks in the park or toy shops and helped them with homework before they would be going back to their father in Minnesota when school was out.

I wrote, *Storm flooded basement. The light outside is beautiful—a light peach color... The sky is more extraordinary up here. Being alone is nice. I look outward through inward, reaching for something, answers or questions, I'm not sure. No one really knows the responsibility of motherhood—not even mothers. It is too much to handle at times. I try to make things as easy and pleasant as I can, perhaps that's bad.* "Mean," *Scott said. I do seem mean when I'm angry, but I don't think I'm expecting too much. Respect and help, honesty and support—all of which I give, or try to give.*

PITTSBURGH

* * *

I can think of many incidents where I should have or certainly could have acted differently towards my children's behavior—being a bit stricter on some things, or more tolerant at times, and not so angry at them for their stubbornness on a particular issue. Other times, I caved in because of my inexperience in motherhood and life—or their charming, sweet natures—as I wondered what I was avoiding. It was years later before I could own up to my addiction.

So, I read Zen and Buddhism books instead. Believing that we choose our parents, I saw myself as the mother that Scott, about to enter the world of drag and makeup, chose. Parents are a role model, like it or not. Children only mirror them, study them, and frequently become like them. I searched for theories on why I drank and did drugs.

My father was a reader and an alcoholic. While growing up I was often told I took after him. I loved to read and became an alcoholic. Is it hereditary, as so many experts claim? Or is it nurture? I make a case for both. Seeing so many relatives showing signs of the family disease, I am convinced there was little I could do to change Scott's course in life, nor would I want to, if it meant he would not have had the careers he had, the life or fun he enjoyed.

Looking back today, my denial of my children's misbehavior and my own addiction was overwhelming. I justified their stealing my marijuana as a way for them to be creative. After all, wasn't that why I smoked pot? To make art? To be inspired? I rationalized it that way. Scott was doing well in school and finishing most of his chores, even if reluctantly. He was drawing, making films, and everyone seemed to love him. I let it slide. He usually got his own way and I found it easier to let him. We both seemed vague about his being gay or not. It didn't seem to matter.

Clearly, I still wasn't ready to be a mother. It was a confusing time for women, especially mothers. We were brought up in one world and had to figure out this new ambivalent one. The independent feminist in me was stronger than the self-deprecating mother I had had.

Nancy Friday wrote in her book *My Mother/Myself* in 1977: "Motherhood doesn't come easily to me.... It isn't because I don't love you. I do. But I'm confused myself.... I feel closer to your age in some ways than I do my mother's. I don't feel that serene, divine, earth-mother certainty you're supposed to that she felt. I am unsure how to raise you. But you are intelligent and so am I. Your aunt loves you. Your teachers already feel the need in you. With their help, with what I can give, we'll see that you get the whole mother package—all the love in the world. It's just that you can't expect to get it all from me." I felt exactly as she had.

The kids loved Pittsburgh, but my art career took precedent and continued to be my main target. It was the reason I left Minneapolis for the East Coast. My rationalization to others and myself was that my only chance at possible success in the art world would be found in New York. Today, I look through sober and recovering-from-addiction eyes, and see that I had been running away from reality. I was navigating my way through substance-fueled narcissism and was making everyone else, including my children, ride in the back seat.

They were often in their rooms, demanding privacy, which Rick and I honored, but I wondered if they were becoming bored in their environment, as I was. After our initial exploration of the area, both Scott and I longed for more excitement. He was arguing with me more and complaining about his chores as he stayed up late, reading or watching TV. I felt the distancing and suspected pot use.

Three months later, in the summer of 1979 we all moved to New York City and were thrilled for this new adventure, yet I wondered, and still do, if I should have moved us.

Scott, c. 1980, PA

Scott, mom and grandma, 1980, UNI

CHAPTER FIFTEEN

NEW YORK CITY

Our new home in Forest Hills, Queens, NY, was a twenty-five-minute, easy subway ride to midtown Manhattan. The house, with thirty-three windows, was even bigger, lighter, and nicer than what we had in Pittsburgh. Rick and I were still working for Gulf Development and now making more money. He was promoted to Regional Manager in Eastern New York while I was working at home as a recruiter. Again, Scott and Kim loved the neighborhood, with its easy access to Central Park or Greenwich Village by subway.

On Mother's Day Scott gave me a vase filled with rare black tulips and prized narcissus. He was fifteen. *Where did he get the money?* I wondered.

On our weekly walk around the new neighborhood, I noticed a lovely house with a picket fence in front of recently cut stems. Horrified, I looked at Scott. He lowered his eyelids, slumped his shoulders forward, and put his hands in his pockets. In a slow, shamed voice, he said, "I'm sorry, I wanted to get you flowers but they were too expensive."

I saw only generosity and charm in my young thief as I admonished him and asked him to deliver an apology note to our neighbor's door later. He agreed, smiling, glad to have pleased me and gotten off so easily. A week went by and nothing had died between us except the flowers. The neighbor and I both forgave him.

I had enrolled them in school and Kim's school, in Forest Hills, skipped her from sixth grade in Pittsburgh to eighth grade in NY. We were all pleased at the time. Rick and I celebrated the new school year by allowing the kids to go to Central Park together, alone. They also went dozens of times to see the *Rocky Horror Picture Show* in the Village, dressing up for the occasion on many nights, usually accompanied by our neighbors' kids, a bit older. It was a safer time.

Scott had fallen in love with New York City at age nine, when our family visited while on a trip east. Now he was excited to be living so near Manhattan. Our neighbor was teaching at Jamaica High School and talked us into enrolling Scott at his school, instead of our neighborhood Forest Hills High. He convinced us there were fewer drugs or dropouts in his school, a few miles away. Scott's grades were excellent or good, but he found Jamaica a drag and continued using marijuana to alleviate the boredom.

I was still restless and unsatisfied after settling in the Forest Hills house, believing my kids were refusing to clean up after themselves and sassing me when I reminded them. Scott stayed out later than allowed and locked his bedroom door more often. I settled for alcohol and pot and my recently set up darkroom.

One night I dreamt of three drug addicts in our house shooting us up with heroin. In the dream we had left on an airplane and were sucked out, falling to the ground. A haystack saved us.

Rick and I were fighting, someone had stolen my pot, and I confronted the kids. Sometimes I smelled oregano or thyme added and suspected Scott was compensating for the missing marijuana. Years later Scott claimed they always found my hidden stash.

"You had concealed it in back of the chicken in the freezer or under the bottom fabric covering the overstuffed chair, but no matter where, we always found it and carefully put the bag back in the same place," he confessed.

I justified Scott's using at fifteen, but I didn't want to admit it.

Paranoid and scared, I wanted to escape, to be free of the responsibility of looking after three kids—including Rick.

The fall of 1979 had started out happily for the four of us. In October, I accepted a job with Portogallo, a photography studio and lab in mid-Manhattan. I quit drinking for two weeks. Threatened by my sobriety, new job, and friends, Rick moved out after weeks of arguing about my working. The breakup had been coming for months. When he was gone, I needed more money. I found another job in Manhattan for a publisher representing commercial photographers.

While I sewed curtains for the French doors, I realized I had not been giving my kids the attention they needed. They had also become distanced by my anger, arguing with me and fighting each other. One evening when I was away at work, Scott decided to take my car out and had an accident. My dream car, a two-year old, fully equipped Volvo with a sunroof, which I had left in the driveway when I took the subway into Manhattan, was badly damaged.

"I'm sorry," my teen-age-son Scott whimpered the next morning when I saw the damage.

"What were you thinking?" I asked. "You're only fifteen, you don't have a driver's license and you never drove in New York City before." I was struggling at being a single mother again.

"But I know how to drive, Dad taught me." He and Kim were going back to Minnesota on summer and winter breaks, and since I'd started working full-time, there was little communication between us. I wondered if he needed more from me.

"You must have dreamt you knew how to drive. Crashing my car and totaling it by plowing into some other guy's new Cadillac is not my idea of knowing how to drive." My son could barely look me in the face.

"It wasn't my fault. The stop sign was covered up by a tree."

I wondered if he was justifying, rationalizing, or mirroring me.

"That's no excuse." I visualized him missing the STOP sign and smashing into the Cadillac with a pimp and five prostitutes.

"But no one was hurt," he pleaded, as if *that* made it okay.

"You were just lucky. Now what am I going to do? The insurance company won't pay because you're an unlicensed driver, underage, and didn't have permission from me to take the car. I have three court summonses against me and I'll have to miss I don't know how many days of work, going to court—plus, I'll have to give up my car because I don't have the thirty-eight-hundred dollars to fix it." I was thinking *Thank God* they didn't get charged with marijuana use or hurt someone else or themselves.

"I'll get a job and pay you back," Scott whimpered.

"Who's going to hire a fifteen-year-old?" I asked.

"MacDonald's will. I'll tell them I'm sixteen." Scott started to cry. My heart warmed from anger to sadness. I slowly got off the chair to move closer to my soon grown-up son and put my arms around him.

"I'm just glad you and Kim are okay. You must have been so scared at the police station." I imagined Scott and Kim sitting in jail together with five prostitutes and their pimp for several hours before I got there. I wondered if he was encouraged to dress up again. He had stopped when we moved to Pittsburgh.

"The women taught me about makeup," Scott said as he smiled. I visualized him with the prostitutes dressed in glitzy sequins and over-the-top makeup, reminiscing about the shows he produced in Minneapolis.

"Come on, let's make some cocoa." I tried not to laugh.

"With marshmallows?" he asked.

"Of course, with marshmallows." First though, I needed a drink.

* * *

After the car episode in November, December 8th was my next worst day ever. A man grabbed at my crotch on the subway going into Manhattan, and I whacked him with my rolled-up Esquire magazine while the crowded commuters laughed. I wanted to leave New York but was determined to stay.

My friend Dee had moved to New York a year before and told me, "The first six months are the worst." But we were all unhappy, and I worried I couldn't control my kids. I proposed they move back to Minnesota.

"Please Mom, don't send us back. I want to stay here. I'm sorry for the car," Scott said.

"Then are you willing to help with the housework and your sister Kim, without resentment?" I bargained after fixing myself a brandy and coke. Rick was gone and I was drinking more.

My kids thought I expected too much from them. I thought I expected too little, unaware of my inability to care for myself properly. I stayed in bed most of the weekend after our talk and wrote in my journal, *The light shines amber/pink constantly—anyway it's all too tiring—wearing me down, wanting to hibernate, wanting to turn lights off and be alone, warm, looking out windows, being at peace.*

Dee was right. A few months later, things looked much brighter. Nineteen eighty brought a beautiful spring to New York. The kids were to spend the summer in Minnesota again, and I began dating, this time seeking men who didn't drink. Our best year in New York went by without much trauma.

Scott with Cecily, c. 1986 - 1988,
PA and UNI

CHAPTER SIXTEEN

FROG DREAM

In the early spring of 1981, I had a dream about a lizard and a frog and wrote in my journal, *The frog was puffing up while I was holding it. Someone said, "He's choking." A lizard came looking for the frog he had attacked. I picked up the frog and he bit me severely on both hands. I put it in a cupboard to save it from the lizard. The dream ended with Scott heaving over me—asthma ...*

My son had started sessions with a gay therapist recommended by my lesbian friend from work. I had shared much of my kids' lives with her before she suggested Scott might be gay, which confirmed my own suspicions. We both thought it would help him to speak with a professional, but I soon felt that it was a mistake. Scott was seventeen and had not yet come out as gay, but he liked the therapist and continued seeing him. I was unimpressed with the young gay (*I assumed*) therapist and believed the frog in my dream was Scott—the lizard, his therapist—and I was bitten trying to save Scott from being gay or not, I didn't know which.

I complained to a friend. "Scott didn't go to school again. He told me he had asthma. I got angry, cried, and said hurtful things. If his problems are because of me, then he shouldn't be with me. His therapist is for him—against me—but I'm for me." I felt as if I was ruining his life.

I wrote in my journal, *Scott may like him—I think he's dangerous. If Scott hates me so much, then he has the option to leave and live with his father. I cannot punish myself any longer.*

My life was in shambles, and I couldn't seem to do anything about it. I believed I'd lost everything with *both* my kids.

Scott hated me for pushing him into choosing between me and his father. I was torn between letting him go to Minneapolis or fighting like hell to save him from a mediocre life in the suburbs with conservative right-wing values. Scott needed to be on his own, yet as his mother I needed to do what I felt was best for him. He seemed to respect his father but rarely shared with me his relationship to him, complaining only about his stepmother. I remembered past scenes of Scott being criticized, reprimanded, punished by Bob for behavior I thought typical of teenage boys. Was he afraid of his father?

"Does he hit you?" I asked.

"No," Scott answered.

"Ignore you or give you that 'silent Norwegian' treatment?"

"No," again.

"Do you think you can get away with staying out late, not doing chores, or not going to school?" I asked him.

Silence.

"Do you want to live in a home [his father's] where you are not allowed to wear your shoes or drink a coke in the living room?" I pleaded.

Scott put his head down and said nothing.

Strange, that lizard dream. I continued to remember it, how I'd taken such care and only when the frog was threatened did I react—through pain, clutching, putting it in the cupboard for protection, and quickly closing the door.

In late March, Scott was sick again. "Asthma," he said, yet he did not have asthma.

I felt responsible and guilty as I wrote, *I love him so and yet I'm destroying him ... Asked him to do something today. He was too tired ... I screamed at him later and said he has two weeks to shape up. I feel he needs an exorcism, from the therapist or me. We're both killing him. This morning I found him hiding in the attic ... Skipping school again. Don't know what to do anymore. I'm sad, feeling lost, guilty.* He always loved school and I wondered and worried why he skipped now. Was he depressed, threatened by the other kids? I needed more support to assist me with helping him. The therapist told me little to nothing.

At my request, Scott's father flew from Minnesota in May to talk with Scott. The next day Bob went to school with Scott and later saw the therapist with and without him. I hoped Bob got at least *some* feeling of what handling him was like. Child-rearing continued to be a mystery to me, while Bob would not share what the therapist said. I could only guess.

Scott had been out of school on twenty-six days since February, and Bob thought I was too hard on him. I disagreed. One hour after his father left, Scott wanted to go out and play Frisbee. I said no.

"You haven't worked on your report and need to make dinner." The kids had each agreed to do one meal a week. Scott left anyway. Later, I wrote, *I cannot go on like this. Scott's not home and I'm supposed to take Bob's bland, arrogant advice to not let it affect me. He doesn't think Scott needs therapy—or even family counseling. As usual, he's blaming me for the problems—I wish he had never come here—purging himself of his own guilt, playing into Scott's hand and believing him. Naturally he finds the answer and fault in me and my response to his son's spoiled and selfish behavior. My life and family are crumbling. I need help. I hugged Scott tonite and told him I love him.*

In June, the wind was blowing and the weather was fine. Before we left for Minneapolis, we were still fighting.

Without any other support, I was certain my son needed stronger discipline. Though we didn't speak about it, the thought of Scott spending the whole year with his father was on our minds. I felt myself giving in to the idea of Scott returning to Minnesota against his wishes.

I started to wonder if I simply could not handle teenagers

while on alcohol and drugs, yet I still resisted facing their *or* my own addictions. Was I deceiving myself? After all, I had raised both of my kids through years of painful teenage dissention. I asked myself, "How the hell did we get here?!"

CHAPTER SEVENTEEN

RETURN TO MINNEAPOLIS

By age seventeen, it became clear that Scott needed more discipline than I could provide, so his father agreed to fly him back to Minneapolis to stay on a temporary basis. He had been smoking pot and skipping a lot of school in New York and his counselor at Jamaica High agreed that Scott would have a better chance of graduating from a high school outside of the city, believing there would be fewer drugs available to him. I found out years later how naïve the counselor had been and learned too late that Scott had skipped as much school in Minneapolis as he had in New York.

Scott did not get along with his father or stepmother, who said she hadn't signed up to be a parent. He told me he moved out to stay with friends. Yet another geographical fix gone wrong. Nevertheless, Scott did earn his diploma from Washburn High School and enrolled at the Minneapolis College of Art and Design, my *alma mater*.

I flew back as often as I could to see how he was doing. Scott was eighteen and living with some grunge rock band members from a group called Loud, Fast Rules, which later became Soul Asylum. He was dressed in torn jeans, a partly shredded T-shirt, and had a punk hairdo—straight up and spiked. He was barely recognizable to me.

While driving north on Central Avenue to the cemetery where my father was buried, I asked Scott, "Do you remember my taking you here when you were ten?" I was on a mission to settle some old bad feelings.

"Vaguely," he answered. "I remember the ride but nothing else."

We were talking about what he was doing now that school was out, and I wanted to know about his new friends. We had not yet spoken of his sexuality, and I was uncertain about my feelings about his being gay. Morally, I had nothing against it. I just thought a homosexual life would be harder on him.

"Do you have any girlfriends?" I asked, not wanting to sound too hopeful. He had brought his best friend Cecily to the family picnic, but I knew they were just friends.

"I noticed that you've only been speaking about guys." I commented.

He shifted in the passenger seat and looked down. "I fall in love with individuals, not genitals," he answered, smiling slightly.

I felt proud of Scott at that moment and thought, *Oh! That makes perfect sense.* Maybe he was *NOT* gay, like I had suspected.

I wanted to say, "What does that mean?" but caught myself and said instead, "What individual are you in love with at the moment?"

"I like my roommate. He's in the band."

"Is he gay?" I asked, my adrenalin rising. The ten seconds it took for him to answer seemed like a lifetime. I was so distracted I made a wrong turn onto a street I was unfamiliar with.

"No. Not yet." He smiled and looked at me. By that point I had pulled over, worried I might hit a parked car or something else.

"Scott ..." I began trying to formulate my words while absorbing my own feelings about the possible truth of his being gay. Fear? Doubt? I didn't know, yet somehow, I always knew this day would come.

"Are we here?" he asked, looking at both sides of the street.

"Not yet, but wait a minute. I'm confused and worried about your drug use," I gladly shifted the subject.

"And living with these band members. Are they doing heroin?" I asked.

"Some are, but don't worry, I don't do that stuff," he answered while he opened the car door. I could tell he was uncomfortable and wanted to end the conversation.

"You know your grandfather, my alcoholic father, died when he was fifty-five, before you were born." Trying to engage his attention, I reached for his hand. "And I'm concerned—" He didn't let me finish.

I felt like a hypocrite, not dealing with my own addictions.

"I know, Mom, but I don't even like alcohol." He pulled his hand away and got out of the car. We walked the half-block silently to the entrance of the cemetery and split up, at his suggestion, to find my father's grave. Scott often shut me out when he was finished talking about a sensitive subject.

"Here it is," he said, somehow knowing exactly where to go.

Using his foot, Scott cleared off the grass clippings and leaves from the simple headstone with his grandfather's name and birth/death dates. Nothing else.

"We should have brought flowers," he said.

"I have something else for him," I replied. Taking out the hard candy from my pocket, I began throwing it on my father's gravestone. The candy shattered in pieces.

"What are you doing?" Scott asked with wide eyes.

"When I was eight years old, on Halloween, my brother and I were at the kitchen table, sorting out the candy we had collected for four hours, two big grocery bags full. My father came home drunk, got mad, and said, 'What's this?' With both his arms he pushed all the candy onto the floor," I explained.

"He beat up my mother and hit your Uncle Tom, and along with that one act of trashing our candy, I never forgave him." I quietly began to explain the suggestion made several months earlier at a gestalt therapist's office when I was seeking treatment for depression.

"She asked if I could look at the empty chair in her office to see what my creative block and sadness was really about. The chair morphed into a brick wall. When she asked what the brick wall represented, my father's image came up. When I told her the Halloween story, it was her idea that I take hard candy and throw it on his grave." I disclosed all this to Scott in a robotic voice, hoping he would understand. Silence.

"Aren't you mad at him for dying before you were born?" I asked my son as I actually wondered if he was angry about my own drug and alcohol use.

"I never really thought about it," he answered. "But give me some of that candy. It looks like fun," He took a handful and threw it at my father's grave with more force than I had.

"This actually feels good!" he said. For me, it was a release I had long waited for. Payback.

We drove home mostly in silence. When we got close to the apartment where he was living, I suggested he join me later at the Art Institute for an exhibit.

"Thanks, Mom, but I need to help my roommate with some instruments for his show tonight. I had a great time today."

He was out of the car in a flash, and I went on my way, feeling a heavy load of confusion, dread, past hurts from *my* father, Scott, *his* father, and all the other men in my life lifted a bit off my shoulders.

At my mother's house, still worried about Scott's drug use, I mixed a drink while wondering about Scott and his roommate.

CHAPTER EIGHTEEN

FAILURE AT MOTHERHOOD

Back in New York, I returned to representing photographers for money, printing in my darkroom and working on my art. My journal entries are filled with dreams, falling in love, and self-pity. On Mother's Day there were *no calls or cards. A proof of failure at motherhood ... Life just seems to go by. I believe in what I'm doing (working) yet deeply disappointed. I need to get help ... the hurt I feel for Scott drags me to a morbid state of mind no one can pull me from ... I cry for all the women who allow themselves to be hurt by others, even their children ... I want to somehow help prevent my kids from the disappointment of it all.*

In a dream I had on May 15th, I was flying around in a helicopter with no blades. Somehow, I was all alone maneuvering the machine, getting directions from those below.

I stopped smoking after a friend was diagnosed with lung cancer. The leader of the New York Cancer Society's three-times-a-week quit-smoking group suggested I try Alcoholics Anonymous in the basement of the same church.

"I can't. They smoke there," I bluntly stated.

But I did began seeing a therapist who asked me to give up drinking for two weeks. I didn't like him, but I knew that alcohol was a problem, so I agreed to stop. I wrote in my journal, *It's helping, but I'm feeling weaker, less in control—a sign of withdrawal?*

In September, after nineteen years, I reconnected with Dave, my first love from tenth grade. He'd given up drinking. *He was beautiful, thin, handsome, grey hair. We drank soda and hinted at going to Vermont together. I told him I never stopped loving him.*

But I had gone back to drinking and recently started with a new therapist, a woman this time, one who had helped many art professionals.

Before Christmas (Scott's favorite holiday) in Minneapolis, I wrote, *Home, coffee and krumkake ... tonight was so very special. I love my family. So dear, close, good, kind and loving to me. They care more than anyone else. Singing Christmas carols around a grand piano with fifteen people ... all of them beautiful ... the feelings were very strong. So far, the happiest time with the family ... no, there are so many happiest times ... every time is special.*

I was almost ready for sobriety.

CHAPTER NINETEEN

ANOTHER MENTOR

I visited Minneapolis in 1983 to see my mother and Scott, who was staying with friends. While shopping at a local bookstore I came across two books, titled *Me* and *If You Want to Write*, by Brenda Ueland. She had lived in New York City, where I was living then, and had moved back to Minneapolis, which I was considering at the time. I bought the books. *Me*, for my mother, and the *If You Want to Write* book for myself. After reading both books I was inspired and wanted more information on this incredible writer who was born in 1891. She had visited the Armory Show in 1913 and while living in Greenwich Village had known radical bohemians like John Reed and Louise Bryant, journalists who became political activists and communists.

I wondered if any in her family were still alive, and to my amazement, she was listed in the phone book. I called the number immediately.

An elderly woman answered, and when asked if she knew the Brenda I was referring to, she said in a high-pitched, older-lady voice, "That's me."

I explained how I had come upon her books at a local bookstore and was quite impressed with her writing and her life. She invited me over to her house, and I accepted, bubbling with excitement.

The cold, crisp air was familiar to me from decades of living in Minnesota. Walking up the steps to her house made me think of my newly acquired admiration for a woman whose life I knew only through her own words. The house, set high on a hill, was covered with ice and snow and looked down on Lake Harriet. I remembered the area from childhood as one where only rich people lived. Had I really been in the same city that she was living in all those many years without knowing her?

I timidly rang the bell and was greeted by her daughter, Gaby, who graciously welcomed me and seemed pleased to have company for her mother.

"Brenda is frail and tires easily but is excited by your phone call and looking forward to meeting you." Gaby said, almost whispering.

I climbed the stairs, feeling Brenda's presence, liking her already, as if I knew her as well as my own mother, daughter, or son.

Brenda was pulling herself up by the steel bars on her hospital bed when I approached. She had a handsome, wrinkled Nordic face with dark, deep-set eyes, and her wide smile lit up the room as I entered. Wild white hair flew in all directions as if the energy from her brain electrified to reach every molecule surrounding her. While devouring my face, she seemed to read me with a burning incandescence.

"Well, there you are. I was waiting for you." She held a delicate hand out, and I hurried over to take it in both my hands.

"I am *so* honored to meet you!"

"And I, you!" She pulled my hands to her heart.

Brenda, at that time, had been bedridden for years. She was ninety-two, enfeebled physically yet sharp mentally. We spoke about her life, my own, our kids. She was interested in Scott's performances and asked about my husband.

"I'm divorced and have no desire for a special man in my life right now," I said.

"If you have no such friend ... well then you must imagine one. Tell me more." She advised or prodded me when she got tired of talking. After several hours, I noticed her nodding out a few times, so I left the room as she fell asleep.

There are moments in one's life that forever define the future. This was one of those moments. Somehow, I knew she would change the course of my life. Still living in New York City at the time, I was unhappy in both my personal and professional situations. I had gone there for my art, much the same as Brenda had in 1914, searching for her future. Instead of professionally pursuing my art, I had recently taken an unsatisfying job at a printing company. I couldn't handle my kids. Scott returned to Minneapolis, and I no longer could ignore my addictions.

Visiting at Christmastime to see my family was a yearly ritual and one that gave me a chance to reflect on the differences between trying to survive in an exciting (if unsatisfying) big city or a more subdued, conservative existence in the Midwest.

When I returned to New York, I went to the 42nd Street Library to look up articles Brenda had written for numerous magazines. With a few changed words from the 1920s articles, the stories could easily have been published today. They were timeless. Reading Brenda's words was like getting advice from a wise creative female who knew the answers to my persistent questions. Should I move back home? How to give up cigarettes or alcohol? How to help Scott get off drugs?

When Brenda wrote about writing, I read it to mean "making art," and certain words from her book advised me, "Forgive me, but perhaps you should write again. I think there is something necessary and life-giving about 'creative work,' a state of excitement. And it is like a faucet: nothing comes unless you turn it on, and the more you turn it on, the more comes ... the rewards were intrinsic, i.e., the enlargement of the soul."

These words promised me a fulfilling life and isn't that why we continue to read? I wanted something better for myself, my children, and my art. I found her books at a time when I needed to make a change in my life, and she seemed to have the knowledge and wisdom I was searching for. Her declarations sang to me from the pages: "When you are writing you will probably think harder than you ever have in your life, and more clearly. But self-consciousness, anxiety, 'intellectualizing' will be untied from you, will be cast off.... The great mystic philosopher Plotinus described 'living in the present' like this: 'In our best and most effective moments, when we really enter into our work, we leave it behind....' In other words, it is when you are really living in the present—working, thinking, lost, absorbed in something you care about very much, that you are living spiritually.... And so once again I have driven home the point: it will be good for you if you will work at your writing."

Now, as I sit here looking out of my window at the still, mostly green leaves waving slightly in the breeze, I think of the many times I visited Brenda during each trip back home, each time a story in itself. I remember her advice to me that I give up photography before she made a phone call to her friend at the Schubert Club to get me a photography job for the prestigious opening of the Ordway Theater in St. Paul. She wanted me to stay in Minneapolis, to create work there and write—maybe a book. She wanted both Scott and me to get off drugs. She wanted Kim to write more.

I remember the spark in her eyes, the warmth of her smile, the chuckle in her voice, and that wild hair—still reaching out for the same energetic connection as I imagined it did those days on the eve of the First World War, when she visited England and France, looking for adventure. Reading her autobiography, I am reminded of the link to so much American history and so many young creative minds in Greenwich Village or Columbia University, and just how much one of these minds can give to the world. But those are *her* stories and *this one* is mine.

Shortly before Brenda passed, I reread her biography, *Me*, and fell in love with several words and "images." I used some of them for a story I wrote: *I was digging in my garden, one of those small gardens with huge, dense weeds in sparse grass under pines. My back was bare to the sun, while my kids were in the house, reading and watching TV. It was the afternoon of a perfectly beautiful summer day. Pulling the roots above the ground, I felt as if I were in church.*

With dirty hands and clear heart, I began singing, harmonizing to a tune in my mind, and my voice rose, giving the day's troubles air and space. The wind was warm and I smelled the sweetness of the earth. No longer addicted to drugs or alcohol, I was free. A cloud moved by and I was chilled for a moment.

There is nothing more truly artistic than to love people, love family ... you have to love something outside and greater than yourself, or you are a goner. Do not care what it is—the sky, a great man/woman, children, or an abstraction like courage, integrity, honor, goodness, or what some people call God. But it must be above your own pleasure and success.

The wind kicked up. And while I dug weeds and thought of these things, my bare shoulders warmly burning from the sun, I had an extraordinary feeling that there are presences in the world, archangels, beings, saints that we cannot see—and they sometimes pull us by the sleeve, saying, "Come; you can really do this."

The rain drove me indoors to my family, my love. Brenda was pulling me home.

I knew I would have to do something, *anything*, to end my reliance on drugs and alcohol. And I believed Scott's growing addiction would not change until *I* changed. Perhaps a trip would inspire us both to recovery.

Scott in Miami. 1984, PA

CHAPTER TWENTY

TRIP TO MIAMI

I sold the family home in Minneapolis in April, 1984. Scott was twenty and Kim was sixteen. I took them both to Miami Beach to celebrate. Scott was hanging out with punk bands and taking art classes but still using drugs. He seemed more himself after having left (or been thrown out) of his father's house. Scott appeared happy when he met us at the Miami airport with bleached-blond hair. Several young gay guys were behind, carrying his bags—his entourage? I asked who they were.

"I have no idea," he smiled. "They just came up to me and asked if they could carry my luggage." To me, and obviously to them, Scott looked like a rock star.

At the B&B the next morning I read a headline in the *Miami Herald*. The Minneapolis Children's Theater Director was indicted for child sexual abuse. Scott had spent a summer at that theater when he was thirteen. He quit the program and never told me why—only, "I don't want to do theater anymore."

We were sitting at a small round table in the kitchen. Sunlight burst through the window as my heart sank. I asked Scott if he had ever been molested by the director.

"What do you mean?" Scott looked at me.

"What do you *think* I mean?" Not wanting to put my imagined deeds into words, I decided to just wait for him to tell me. He certainly knew what I meant and by now, no longer innocent to sexual behavior, could answer if he had been molested.

After a long delay while looking out the window, he replied, "No." Scott lowered his head, meaning he did not want to talk about it or was hiding the truth. Had he wanted me to figure out what was going on? Did he expect me to guess his thoughts as I had done previously?

"I'll fix some breakfast," I said, leaving the table. He wouldn't tell me. He never did. I felt sad that I hadn't protected him. I often felt that.

Scott seemed to have decided long ago that whatever had happened, he would just embrace the imperfection of certain elders. Continuing into adulthood, he endured whatever emotional wounds he encountered and seemed to put them out of his memory. It was similar to what I had experienced from alcohol and drugs. I carried missing pieces for years, never telling, as I tried to hide any negative effects. If others don't know, then maybe it didn't happen or even affect us. Or was it just more denial?

But we were in Miami. The bright sun was shining on an aqua ocean. I had the familiar thought that everything could be fixed. We changed the subject.

After a day on the beach, we drove down to Key West. I had splurged on a fancy B&B. Scott played the grand piano while Kim, in a bathing suit, joined me at the pool. She had become a beautiful tall, thin young woman with long straight hair that turned heads—gay women and men alike. I hoped that she and I would bond during this trip and beyond. I really believed it was a good vacation for all of us.

Back in New York, Kim and I were not getting along. The fights got fiercer, and I was missing work. Kim's friend was stabbed one night, and I went to her school for advice. "Help her pack a bag and let her go," the counselor said.

"Go where?" I asked. She shrugged her shoulders in silence. I went home and called Bob.

"Sorry, Susan and I cannot have Kim live with us," he said. My sister Nancy offered to care for her in her and her husband Jim's house in the suburbs of Minneapolis. They were still raising the last of their six kids in Catholic school. I was grateful and hopeful.

Kim moved into her aunt's house the summer before her senior year, while I began a plan to move back to Minneapolis. The next day in the subway I was asked by a crazy lady, "What country do you think you're in and how did you get here?" That seemed to explain everything to me. It was the last straw. I would try to save myself and my kids by moving back home.

Cecily and Scott, c. 1986, PA

Scott, c. 1986, PA

CHAPTER TWENTY-ONE

RECOVERY AND ADDICTION

I packed up the house in Forest Hills, New York, and returned to Minneapolis in the fall of 1984 to be with her. Kim would be entering her last year of high school. The family came over for a welcome-home party in our new twentieth-floor apartment, a block from the Walker Art Center by Loring Park, near downtown Minneapolis. My mother, brothers, sister, their spouses, Scott, and Kim—all ten of us—sat around the dining room table. We were laughing, reminiscing and telling stories when I must have blacked out. I awoke in the middle of the night with my head on the table. Everyone was gone.

Wow! I realized my enablers were blind and would be of no help with my own recovery from dependency. Most of them were drinkers, some heavy drinkers—it was a curse on our family. Months went by before I finally took the first step to recovery in an out-patient rehab program near Scott's apartment. After three sessions a week for five weeks and a few AA meetings, I thought I was all better and believed I could help my son get off drugs.

A few years after our trip to Miami, Scott was in bed in a messy basement apartment in a not-so-nice neighborhood of Minneapolis. He had recently moved there after being evicted from his previous place. Since moving out of his father's house, he'd had several apartments. Books, clothes, plastic bags filled with who-knows-what were littered around him. I could tell he was high.

"I brought you some food," I said, approaching him. He pulled himself partially up and looked around to see if there was anything he didn't want me to see. Drug paraphernalia? Needles? Powders? I chose not to look away or at the areas he was scanning but kept my eyes on my once-beautiful twenty-two-year-old son. He was at his lowest point, emaciated, with dirty hair—looking at me with absolute indifference. I had heard from friends he'd been a heroin addict for two years.

I wondered how he had paid for his drugs. He'd dropped out of school, had no job, and was killing himself alone in this horrible ritual. It felt like the saddest moment in my life.

I entered a treacherous hole in hell, where there was *nothing* I could do except ask others for support. After many calls to friends and rehab centers, I found some options and pleaded with Scott to go for help. We discussed his property, which had been piled in a corner since he moved in: a birdcage, suitcases filled with art supplies, drawings of heads and faces, wigs, makeup, a few childhood keepsakes, and lots of clothes.

"Where will it all go when you're in treatment?" I asked, hoping it sounded like a done deal. It wasn't. He had not committed at the intervention I'd arranged earlier. I offered to get a storage unit and handle the details while I uncovered the food I had brought to him. As I approached, he looked away. "I'll eat it later, Mom, thanks," he said. I held my total defeat inside like a stone.

Too many times previously, I had tried pleading with him to stop using, seek treatment, or simply look at the brochures I had brought him.

"This will pass," I thought yet knew he wouldn't listen to my own experiences of recovery again. I still needed so much help myself.

In the darkness of that room, I could see the fall from grace of my once-beautiful, strong-but-gentle prince as he dozed off. Scott had lost himself. He was there but not there. I attempted to trust he would return after his anger faded from the shadows of some long-held resentment, ending the sadness and pain in his heart. Or he would fall further and come to seek help on his own. If I kept our deep-rooted love tight enough inside myself, maybe it could overcome the hurt we both suffered.

I took his struggle with me as I left. Saying, "Goodbye," quietly, almost whispering. Out in the cold, I prayed the darkness that weighed us down would lift. I'd wanted to hear him agree to going into treatment. That night I believed it was impossible. My son had gotten hooked on heroin while hanging out with a grunge rock band. I gathered many friends and family members along with a professional coordinator to attend several interventions. Finally, after two treatment centers, we were successful. Our leader Mary was the key component. She would not let us leave the room until Scott agreed to get sober.

Scott gave up drugs and stopped drinking in January, 1988 at a hospital in Wilmer, Minnesota, more than a hundred miles outside of Minneapolis, away from his dealer and druggie friends. He wrote to me his first week there. I had moved back to New York after the final intervention. "I saw a social-psychologist today—she was great, we both had a good time doing my assessment—she told me I am an arrogant, manipulative son of a bitch who is very smart, has lots of talent, and will probably go a long way if drugs don't get in the way. I just smiled and nodded yes. She was interested in the close parallels between you and me and how my father is kind of the opposite."

At Scott's request, I spoke to his counselor, Don.

"Where do I start? There is alcoholism on both sides of his family. I've been sober now two years and eight months." I explained.

"That's great! Congratulations. When did Scott start using drugs?" Don asked.

"I think he started smoking pot around age thirteen. My friends and I smoked and drank,"

"What about school? Was he a good student?"

"When he applied himself he got As but his behavior changed at fifteen, after he smashed up my car. I suspected drugs."

"Any reason in particular?"

"I was drinking and using more drugs, plus my parenting skills were at a low point. At eighteen, he was too much for me to handle so he went to live with his father in Minneapolis."

"Did that help?" I knew Don had spoken to Scott's psychologist and possibly his father.

"Not really. Scott and I have always been close. His rebellious nature probably came from me, but his stubbornness came from both his father and I—two Leos."

"Are you blaming your and Scott's drug use on your astrology sign?"

I had no answer for that so changed the subject.

"My hope now is for him to accept his powerlessness over drugs and trust the higher power concept. I think he also needs to deal with family stuff and his sexuality."

"Any other concerns?" Don asked.

"Yes, I'm concerned that he'll get depressed and bored by his lack of structure and inability to do art. I'm hoping that his pleasant manipulative manner won't fool the counselors. I know it'll most certainly gain him allies among the residents. He's a very popular young man. I'm also afraid if he's confronted too much, he'll leave, like he did at Eden—his first treatment center. There's a fine line with him—when he's had enough criticism, he runs away. Please try to give him more structure, especially on weekends."

It was a three-month program, but after two months, as expected, Scott wanted to leave. I offered him a round trip ticket to New York if he finished treatment. It worked! He stayed in the hospital. A few weeks later his doctor called to say Scott had swollen neck glands and it could be HIV. The blood test would be back in a few weeks. I went into a daze, feeling devastated as I walked to work through Central Park, barely noticing the trees and flowers in bloom, overwhelmed at the possibility that Scott may be infected with AIDS.

Would I lose my son? Could I care for him during the horrendous stages of the disease? Several of my gay friends had died, or were sick. All were terrified of catching this plague. I pleaded with them to be celibate. My preoccupation felt like a cloud over me, heavy with rain, never quite letting up. I remember only waiting and crying during the few weeks that seemed like months. AIDS was devastating gay communities worldwide, and New York City in particular was losing talented lives on a daily basis. My wanting Scott in New York with me was a mother's naïve wish to protect a son who may have gotten this disease in Minneapolis, a seemingly safe city compared to New York. Besides, I'd had unfavorable past experiences there myself with drugs, alcohol, and relationships.

The diagnosis was negative for HIV! I was so relieved! Instead, Scott had contracted Hepatitis C by sharing needles with someone in the band. Hep C, at that time, was almost as scary as a diagnosis of AIDS. The good news was that if he gave up drugs and alcohol and kept clean, he would be okay. I was relieved yet wondered if Scott could do that. We agreed he would stay with me a few weeks until he got a job and apartment or share. He wrote to me before completing the program: "I've done a lot of work on control issues here. I know a lot of my controlling personality comes from you as well as my father. I have this fear that you will try to control my sobriety. You told me there are going to be rules when I stay with you. I can deal with not using in your home and not being there under the influence of anything—but anything else, like having to tell you where I will be at all times. That is trying to control my sobriety."

Scott included a pamphlet on controlling and one on letting go, along with some drawings, one a self-portrait with tears on his cheeks. I was touched, happy he'd given me artwork.

In April, 1988, after successful drug treatment, Scott returned to New York, the city he so loved. I was sharing with a friend an apartment on Fifth Avenue overlooking Central Park and working at an upper-East Side art gallery. We all agreed Scott would stay in our apartment temporarily. He flew to New York, using only one way of the round-trip ticket I bought him. He was twenty-four.

I called my AA sponsor after Scott was settled. "Scott's been here three weeks. He's decided to stay and now he's driving me nuts with his laziness, his 'life owes me' attitude. He's not going to meetings either. I'm scared he has or will start using again, I don't trust him. And I feel guilty because of that. My roommate has befriended him, suggesting we give him another chance after I told him he had to leave tomorrow."

"Are you going to meetings?" my sponsor asked.

"Yes, I'm going to AA, Alanon, ACA (adult children of alcoholics)—and tomorrow, a Nar-anon (narcotics anonymous) meeting, but I still can't make a decision. It's so hard. I'm sure if I kick him out, he will go to a friend who uses. But he goes there many nights already, and I believe he'll use anyway. My serenity is being affected."

"If I were you, I would ask him to leave," she said.

"I can't detach or let go of the fear, and my intuition says 'get him out,' but my mother-guilt allows him to stay. He's angry because one of my conditions to his staying is two meetings a week."

"He agreed to that, right?"

"Yes, but he says I'm trying to control his sobriety. I say I'm trying to control my own. I don't want to be around recovering people who are not prioritizing their recovery. It hurts so much to see him lying on the couch, knowing he has anger towards me and pain from recovery that he's not dealing with. I try explaining early sobriety to him."

"How's that worked out?"

"Not so much. I encourage him to express his anger, but I'm also angry. I feel he's using me, taking for granted my 'mother' status, taking advantage of my roommate and our living situation on Fifth Avenue. We work our asses off to pay for that place. He contributes nothing."

My sponsor, who had no children, was silent. I took that to mean she had no more advice.

A week later I wrote to a friend, "My son is here, living with me and he's doing well. Last night he had a dinner date with the director and star of *Sticky Fingers*, a new film. I'm hoping he finds his own place soon—we haven't lived together since he was a teenager."

To a second friend, I wrote, "Scott's lethargy and his not going to meetings upsets me. I'm grateful that he's here in New York, but I see myself procrastinating when I look at him lying down. I think I need to kick him out."

It seemed to me that he would never leave. A few weeks later, since I wasn't able to listen to advice from anyone, I wrote a third whiny letter to a friend I met in my own recovery group: "Scott is using our apartment like a hotel to fall back on. Tomorrow he moves in with the Cuban lover he met in NA. He uses people, and I need to say 'no' to him. It's hard, but Nar-Anon is great. They talk about us being codependent and maybe sicker than them—true. Three years of sobriety have shown me that alcohol and pot were just the tip of the iceberg. Relationships are so hard and yet I want one so badly each day."

Alcohol and drugs were gone from my life, yet other addictions began to resurface.

Scott with my mother and cousins at his
second birthday, Minneapolis, 1965, PA

Scott, c. 1990 – 2010, PA

Scott in glasses with Mom, Jezebel, Flo Kennedy and author (bottom), c. 1995 – 2006, UNI

Scott with Mom, Willow and Castle, c. 1996 –
2006, UNI, PA and Jennifer Bong

Scott, Mom, and orchids, f. 2006 PA and UNI

Scott, Mom and Godmother, Heidi, Paris, c. 1990, PA and UNI

Scott, Mom, Kim, c. 1989 – 2010, PA and UNI

Invitations to shows, c. 1989 – '94

Top left: Misty and Misdemeanor, c. 1989 – '94, UNI and PA
Top right: Misty signing My Comrade magazine, 1991, Leonard Drindell
Bottom left: Misty at home, East Village, c. 1990 – '92, UNI
Bottom right: Taboo with Misty, c. 1990 – '93, UNI

Top left: Misty, c. 1990 – '93, PA and UNI
Top right: Misty, c. 1990 – '93, UNI
Bottom left: Misty in Blue wig, c. 1991, UNI
Bottom right: Misty with Leonard and Jed, c. 1994, UNI

Misty, Taboo and Jimmy Paulette, dressing,
NYC 1991, Nan Goldin

Scott traveling and at home, c. 1995 – '97,
UNI and PA

Misty with Jimmy Paulette at parade, NYC,
1991 UNI and Nan Goldin

Joey Gabriel with Misdemeanor, Misty at parade, Misty in blond wigs, c. 1991 – '93, Linda Simpson

PART II.

Light:

* * *

Ruby-Lipped Orchid, *Cattleya labiata.*
Large crimson epiphyte growing up
in trees where light is plentiful. The plant has long leaves
with a tough consistency.

Scott and me at Caffe Strada, Central park, 1988, UNI

CHAPTER TWENTY-TWO

SOBER IN NEW YORK CITY

Kevin, a friend of mine from Minneapolis, had recently moved to New York to open a coffee-cart business called *Caffe Strada* in midtown. He needed help at the Central Park location and hired Scott.

It was a sunny, warm day and the park was in full bloom as I walked the fifteen blocks to Sixtieth Street. Scott was wearing a black hat and sleeveless white T-shirt. It was the fall of 1988.

"*Un cappuccino per favore,*" I ordered in my best rehearsed Italian accent.

"Hi Mom." Scott smiled as he pulled the lever. "You're my tenth customer today." It was still two hours before noon. "My quota is fifty cups, and I should reach that by early afternoon."

"This coffee is GREAT!" I exclaimed loudly, hoping others would stop and buy as I remembered the courage and love between us that had made this possible.

My caterer-roommate also gave Scott service jobs while he went to Narcotics Anonymous (NA) meetings. Scott's new friends in the program became a great resource, helping him find other jobs and housing. They offered the support he needed to navigate the city sober.

These new friends, colleagues, and mentors were mostly gay men who grew up like Scott—creative, curious, determined children who did not buy into the roles and rules of traditionalist society. Gender conformity was the prototype parents wanted for them but new role models were on TV. *All in the Family*, *Mary Tyler Moore*, *Maude*, and *Golden Girls* were our favorite shows. Times were changing. The shift from post-World War II conservatism to modern experimentation was the new cool. Scott moved on from the days when cousins and friends followed him into a made-up world of his imagination. He was now part of a talented, fun-loving group of young, hip, downtown New Yorkers, an innovative tribe of like-minded comrades.

After moving to the East Village in his mid-twenties, Scott house-sat for Tabboo! (Stephen Tashjian), the artist and drag performer who considered Scott's drag identity, Miss Demeanor, his new protégé—according to an invite Scott sent me from Mars, a gay club on the West Side Highway at Thirteenth Street, advertising, "A dazzling display of disco love."

Scott found an apartment above a church on East Sixth Street, between Avenues C and D, where he met and shared with Josiah Howard, a writer and drag performer who took the name "Coffee," due to his being half black and half white. They furnished the apartment with discarded items found on the streets each month, left by people who were moving. Their cool creativity added to the décor. Josiah remained Scott's best friend until the end, Skyping with him on the phone almost every day.

The East Village edginess became a playground for Scott's ingenuity and a stage for his next production. Along with Josiah, Jimmy Paul, Tabboo!, and other like-minded queens, they dressed up together for shows, often at Boy Bar or The Tunnel, but mostly at the Pyramid Club.

Miss Demeanor was the skinny drag queen who would lip sync hoarse black voices like Eartha Kitt, Patti LaBelle and Dinah Washington. She was paid $50 a night for a show and $150–1000 for a private party. Her own makeup was so successful, that Scott was soon asked by other drag performers to do *their* makeup.

Scott's friend from Narcotics Anonymous, Leonard Drindell, 40, and his partner, Joe, 50, lived nearby. Leonard was a free-lance stylist and photographer, and Joe was a floral designer. They lived in a fifth-floor walkup in a grungy old tenement building on First Street, just off First Avenue—a run-down neighborhood where Soho meets the Bowery and the East Village. Their bathtub was in the kitchen, covered with a hollow core door when used as a dining table. The toilet was in the hall, shared by other apartments on the floor. Scott was excited to meet these like-minded, creative ex-drug addicts and happy to house-sit for them when they traveled to Florida. I was invited over once.

"Mom, look at this!" Scott pointed to the covered bathtub. "Let me show you ... come over here ... what do you think of that?" He was animated as he took me through the sensual and delightful apartment styled with treasures collected from travels or just junk off the street. Scott showed me walls covered with thrift shop art, fashion magazine pages, and Leonard's and other flea market artworks—while telling stories of their collaborations, their mutual love of kitsch, drag, and anything odd. Joe brought home huge bouquets of flowers he arranged for the lobby of the Doral Hotel twice each month, and bouquets of dried or fresh blooms that surrounded their cozy, intimate seating areas. Upscale home magazines like *Architectural Digest* recently showed interiors that looked exactly like their place did in the late eighties and early nineties. Scott came alive in this unusual environment, so different from the one he'd grown up in.

Leonard introduced Scott to Quentin Crisp, the self-proclaimed effeminate writer and actor who lived in a tiny room nearby. They had Quentin over to breakfast on Sundays in one or the other of their eclectic apartments and listened to Crisp recount his life while they experimented with makeup and crossdressing. A role model to Scott, eighty-year-old Crisp realized he should have been a trans woman rather than a gay man. Before dying, he wrote, "My life would have been much simpler as a result."

"You will survive if you believe in yourself." Quentin told Scott.

Scott and Leonard stayed friends until they died. Even after his partner Joe died, and Leonard moved to Fort Lauderdale, they kept in touch. I always felt Joe was a suitable father figure and Leonard was the dilettantish, creative older brother that my son never had. Scott saved hundreds of postcard collages that Leonard had made and sent over the years, most with cut out pictures he had taken of Scott in drag.

The last trip Scott took was to see my husband David and me in a rented condo on the beach in Fort Pierce, Florida, in March, 2014. He brought along a young friend from England. Luke Abby, twenty, loved drag and had been lured to New York at age seventeen to be a stylist after doing fashion design work for Lady Gaga. Leonard was ill but wanted to see Scott, and Luke wanted to see Miami. Scott rented a car to drive south from Fort Pierce, stopping for a few days in Fort Lauderdale on their way. The three multigenerational men played dress-up in the theme of Grey Gardens after watching the famous documentary about the two aging eccentric relatives of Jackie Onassis. They took photographs in Leonard's overgrown garden. Scott was glad to see his longtime friend. He staged and dressed Luke, Leonard, and himself in long scarves and see-through dresses for the camera.

A few months after they spent those magical days together, Leonard learned Scott had passed away. He stopped eating and three weeks later was found dead.

CHAPTER TWENTY-THREE

WHY DRESS UP?

I often wondered how Scott became Scott—how he chose his course. Things that were part of the past now speak loudly to me. He allowed that past to return at the end of his life, by wanting to do drag again. He had stopped in 1994 when his makeup career took off. The love he had for me, his sister, and all the women and girls in his life led to dressing up, putting on makeup, and, yes, adding a sense of theater, where a perfect mirror into another life evolves into the curious identity of womanhood.

Ru Paul, like Scott, wanted to be David Bowie. All three attempted to break down walls by using drag as a launch-pad to free their creative souls. "We are all born naked and the rest is drag. When you become the image of your own imagination, it is the most powerful thing you could ever do, like God playing dress up," Ru wrote. While they shaped identities in front of the mirror, with their confidence in control, each passed from male into female knowing that they had never been completely masculine or totally feminine.

I was delighted to meet Scott's friend Ru in a home supply store in Chelsea. Scott was there to buy bedding, and I'd gone off to the kitchen department. After a few minutes, Scott reappeared while I was looking at a strainer. I knew whatever I picked he would buy for me.

"Mom, I want you to meet my friend." I followed him down

a narrow aisle. At the end was the most beautiful, tall black man wearing men's clothing and a welcoming smile.

"So, *you're* Scott's mom? I've heard so much about you—and I see how Miss Demeanor got her beauty and grace," Ru said, as he held both my hands.

I think now, so many years later, that Ru might have been at the end of an aisle for a reason. He was avoiding the white people shopping, avoiding the disdainful looks and deprecating comments that would arise if they witnessed us embracing as we met. I remembered how racism has always been our country's open, ugly secret, along with homophobia and sexism. "Drag is there to remind culture not to take itself too seriously. All of this is illusion.... The people who do drag are people who dance to the beat of a different drummer," Ru Paul wrote.

We cling to memories that define us but what defines us is often in our imagination. I periodically visit the unreal space where Scott is still alive, smiling, and imagine his voice explaining to me why he dresses up. He tells me—*I saw beauty as power so I wanted to be beautiful. I became a queen casting a spell, knowing who I was by only putting on a mask. As I moved on stage and danced to Respect or other powerful songs from a female performer, I fulfilled the persona I longed for. I became someone else.*

I wonder if it was from watching me when he was a toddler as I went through my closet—pulling out dresses, skirts, pantsuits—holding up different colored fabrics in front of him before the mirror. I remember a black dress with fringe and how that fringe twirled when I held it in front of me as I turned right, left, around, back. The movement of the layers mesmerized Scott while I moved back and forth. We were listening to music and I was dancing. I had the dress on and Scott was in my arms as I turned—swaying, laughing.

I sit back on the cozy overstuffed, shabby-chic sofa in my now-favorite writing spot, swooning with this picture in my mind.

WHY DRESS UP?

It seems real, even though I have conceived our conversation. I hear him again—*Another time, maybe I was six or seven, you were in your sewing room just across the hall from my room. As the sewing machine purred, I went in to see yards of the silky, pink-paisley fabric draped over your shoulder, across your lap, and flowing onto the floor. You were making leisure home-wear, a pantsuit, with wide, generous bell-bottoms. You smiled and said, "Come with me," Slipping the pantsuit over your shorts, you took my hand and we were twirling.*

When I hear a certain song on the radio, I remember those sunny, warm summer days when Scott watched me put on makeup in front of the mirror in our purple, black, and white bathroom with the Renaissance Michelangelo shower curtain that had nudes on it. The curtain was swaying in the breeze.

And still in my imagination, Scott walked towards the couch and leaned close to me. *It seemed to me my mom was a magician, so beautiful—with dark eyes, bright pink lips—as you pulled your long hair up, twisting it to clip on top of your head, then letting it down.*

"Which way?" you asked me.

"Down," I told you before you went out.

I thought then that my life would begin when I could dress up like you, when I could put on makeup and be beautiful. Many times, I went through your closet, trying on a silk skirt that I wore as a dress, your formals from high school proms, or the lady-of-the-court dresses that Grandma made for you. If the babysitter would let us, Kim and I put on a show for her with makeup—me as Charlie Chaplin or a damsel in distress. It was our favorite game while you and Dad were away. I knew that when he was home, I couldn't dress up or put on lipstick. He was always furious and punished me when he saw me in dresses or makeup.

As I watched Scott's father take away his doll or stuffed monkey when he was a toddler, I felt injured. When I asked Bob why, he'd say, "No son of mine is going to play with a doll!" While Bob cringed at Scott's feminine mannerisms I sunk into self-judgement. After all, *I* was dressing up and putting on makeup. Was Bob also ashamed of me?

As I saw it, Scott was commemorating womanhood. Eighteen when my son was born, I knew nothing of raising a child. I started out as an artist, photographer, and writer naïve to parenthood. It seemed fine and natural that my creative son wanted to imitate me. I often wonder if Scott would have become a drag performer had I not celebrated him for the shows he created as a child or if he had not had role models like David Bowie, or *Laugh-In* skits, or my feminist friends, or the ferment of the sixties and seventies—Viet Nam, Nixon, Marilyn, or Kennedy. He was a sponge, soaking up values, ideals, images and galaxies of possibilities for alternative ways to live.

Why is it embarrassing to some people who see a man or boy dressed as a girl or holding a baby doll? It seems to provoke a different feeling, I think, than seeing a girl or woman dressed in men's clothing. We were called *tomboys*, and *that* was acceptable. Why the difference? I believe the answer reaches into the entirety of the misogynistic, homophobic society we live in. If we could answer that embarrassment, we might get to the heart of the gender gap. The LGBTQ issues of today seem so different from the past, more out in the open. Chauvinism, fear of sensitivity or feminine traits in men are in the daily news. I wish I knew today what Scott thought about all this.

My feelings of joy in Scott's drag personas came from my feminism and my experiences meeting women I admired as much as or more than the men in my life. While Scott's father tried to raise his son to *not* be a girl, I objected and enjoyed seeing the feminine come out in him.

Since toddlerhood, Scott had closely watched me photograph myself and other women dressed up. He became a drag queen. He helped me plant in the garden and became an expert on plants, including orchids and other exotic species, knowing the botanical names for all two hundred in his collection. He listened to music I put on the turntable and became an accomplished classical pianist, playing the Bach, Chopin, and Mozart that I loved. Now he was teaching me.

Scott, c. 2000, PA

Scott as Misdemeanor and Misty, c. 1988 – 1991, PA and UNI

CHAPTER TWENTY-FOUR

DRAG

The first time I saw Scott perform in a professional drag show, before he identified as Misty or Miss Demeanor, was at a club in Tribeca, on Hudson Steet in lower Manhattan. It was 1988. He had already performed at Wigstock, the end-of-summer gay celebration in the Village, but that was not paid, professional work. A printed invitation arrived and I invited my friend Perry from Minneapolis. Perry was in New York to protest with ACT UP, demanding more money for AIDS research. I also called my friend Debbie, a photographer and photo dealer, who had known Scott since our Minneapolis days.

I was nervous to see my son outside the safety of our home, worried he would be judged by strangers, and I felt our friends would protect Scott from unruly or loud homophobic drunks.

Perry and I arrived early, and immediately went to the table where Debbie sat with a big smile. I hugged her, so happy she came.

"I got to see him!" she exclaimed and by the glow on her face, I knew he looked terrific. We ordered cokes all around. Perry was my sponsor in AA, and Debbie rarely drank. Within a few minutes, Scott came out in a long, blond wig with braids, over-the-top makeup, big lips painted a shocking pink, too-big falsies, a tight, sequined, silver sleeveless top over a miniskirt, leggings, and high heels. Because of the braids, I thought of a German bar maid. Had he a name for herself, I imagined it would be Big Boobs

Brunhilda. Scott had a seltzer with us, chatted cheerfully, then calmly went onstage. I shot a roll of film and kept looking at my friends and the audience for their approval. Scott was beaming at my apparent pleasure. Seeing smirks on a few shocked faces, I turned away from them, not wanting any unappreciated response. I totally ignored those strangers who did not have a smile and/or look of adoration. How dare they judge my gorgeous son!

Lip-syncing to the words by Patti Labelle, Cindy Lauper, and other favorite singers of the time, my son moved like a tiger pacing the space, determined to own her territory. With pouting lips and grand gestures of arms and hands, she transcended her role as a man.

Scott's friend, Cecily, who had moved to NY from Minneapolis to be with him, came in with a shaved head, a large ring in her nose, and huge earrings dangling to her shoulders. We waved her to our table up front, and Scott moved more loosely in her presence as if he had been coached by her and wanted to impress. They were best friends, and it was obvious he was comforted by her presence. I felt uneasy. How would I feel if this became his profession? I thought drag queens a bit over the top and somewhat embarrassing, but in my son, I saw a performer *playing* a drag queen. He had too much class, too much esteem for women to caricature or make fun of them for how they dressed or moved. I saw Scott celebrating women and his own feminine side and felt proud, seeing him as a Princess, not a Queen—not yet. We all loved the show.

Perry had written the introduction to his book, *The Color of Light*, about the old native North American Indian tradition called *heyoehkah*, or sacred clowns, people within the tribe who "did things differently"—who challenged people's thinking and shook them up. Their function was to keep their people from getting stuck in rigid ways of thinking and living. They were also known as "contraries" because they lived backwards. They walked backward, danced backward, everything they did was contrary to the norm. Heyoehkah were often gay, and we discussed their similarities to drag after the show.

"It reminded me of a powwow. What a perfect way to celebrate gayness," Perry said.

"How so?" I asked. We were walking up Hudson Street in Tribeca after the show. Perry stopped and looked down to ponder my question.

"I saw Scott draw us into a sacred community as circles of light swirled around him, symbolizing the shadow of God, reminding us of our spiritual center."

Shivers ran down my spine as we started to walk again.

"I just saw him dancing in the light," I replied, wondering about those circles.

Scott with Perry, c. 1989 and other gigs, c. 1990, PA and UNI

Author with David Ekroth, Texas, c. 1990,
Selfie by David Ekroth

CHAPTER TWENTY-FIVE

LOVE ADDICTION

I didn't want to dwell on the past or the future; one was gone forever and the other was not yet here. I decided to live in the moment and let go of past insecurities and resentments. I had made many bad decisions in choosing a partner but continued to look for relationships.

Scott was newly sober, had just begun his professional drag career, but I was still addicted to love. After two years of no drugs or alcohol, I met a man through my friend Ivory.

I wrote in my journal: *It was one of those days, like when you were a teenager, and your friend had done homework with the boy you wanted to date, but she just used that as an excuse to spend time with him and then said, "I don't understand why you're so mad." That kind of day, when I needed to fulfill a commitment of bringing friends to a fundraiser I had promised to attend that was not really much of anything, but I wanted to show my support.*

My disposition turned for the worse until I met Ivory's friend Mamood from Uganda, and, as usual when meeting someone I'm attracted to, I ignored him all the way up to the International House. Later, we were back at Ivory's discussing AIDS and art and what our plans were for the evening. We were going to watch Skot dance at the Pyramid. [Scott spelled his name that way on artwork, letters, notes, and postcards for a short time in his twenties. I believed he wanted a new identity, a sober start.]

Mamood was curious without much passion, and that intrigued me, so I flirted a bit while walking over to Tomkins Square, brushing my arm on his, talking politics and social problems, thinking "he cares" and is attending to me, not Ivory or Martha. When we got to the club and Martha & I danced, it interested me to know if he was watching. I looked over a few times but he didn't seem to rivet his eyes on me. After we watched Skot dance, I took Mamood back to the floor, and we started dancing closely together. When I'd watched him dancing with Martha, he hadn't even been looking at her, nor dancing sexy, but now it was if we were mesmerized by each other and moving so well together, no more than an inch apart, which heightened the sexual energy. Then I knew we wanted each other right there and thought it was obvious to everyone around.

That night felt like a Fellini film at the Pyramid Club as I started to photograph Skot dancing in drag. A drunk bald man with fat lips came up to me and asked "Is that a girl or a boy?" He was pointing at Skot. I said, "I don't know," but should have said, "both" or "neither."

Patti Smith wrote, "As far as I'm concerned, being any gender is a drag."

Later, in the car Mamood and I touched each other's backs, our legs touching, faces brushing and wanting so much to just hold, kiss, and make love. I needed air and suggested we go out, and we decided to walk. The daze I was in was really an agony of desire, and I was out of control and just following whatever was decided, which was to get a cab, go home and, holding hands, wonder.

"How will this end?" Ivory asked, "Are you going to take this boy home with you?" Well, the answer was out instantly, "I'd love to," Later, in my apartment, we stood close again, kissing as we unbuttoned each other's clothes.

Mamood returned to Uganda and within weeks, I found another love interest, a new obsession. A different drug.

LOVE ADDICTION

* * *

"I produced *Phantom of the Opera* on Broadway." Lewis said, when I first met him in 1988. I was eager to introduce him to Scott, thinking he would cast him in a play.

"I thought Andrew Lloyd Webber produced that," My roommate Carla said. But charming, egocentric, manipulative and passive aggressive, lying Lewis was just the kind of guy I was attracted to, so it didn't matter if he lied.

I wrote in my journal: *Once again the should-be-familiar-by-now infatuation fills me with a sweet euphoria, creeping over my entire body and soul, as if my heart is filled and needs more space. Anticipation leaks out of me. I wait for the phone to bring me encouraging offers of our next meeting.*

"I'm so very drawn to you. I want to kiss you, make love to you," Lewis cooed. We flirted with each other while courageously walking in Central Park at night, talking about intimacies.

Weeks went by after our first perfectly amazing date, with no calls from him or messages on the answering machine. Another great sensual evening followed by more weeks of nothing. I was drawn to oddballs, but this was too much. I decided to *not* introduce him to my son.

"Pathological," Flo said when I described him.

I had found support at AA, Alanon, Naranon, and Artists Anonymous groups. When a friend suggested I try a Women Who Love Too Much meeting in an upper-East Side church basement, I hoped it would help. Seventy well-dressed, intelligent, businesswomen sat in a circle sharing similar love/sex addicted stories. It was so sad. Whining, privileged women with no solutions offered. I never went back.

I had little control over this new obsession with Lewis so did what I was best at, running away. I planned a trip out of the country. Scott was settled in the East Village starting his drag career, and Kim was in Montpellier, France, studying French.

I saved for this trip for months and looked forward to bonding with my daughter. I hoped also to put the relationship with Lewis behind me.

I flew to Paris, rented a car and drove the seven hours south to Montpellier. After a few days there, Kim, her girlfriend Nancy, and I would begin our two-week trip to Spain and Portugal.

First, we would visit the writer Lawrence Durrell in Sommières. I had read his books twenty-five years earlier on the boat trip down the Mississippi River. My friend Susan had lived with Durrell in Paris when they were both young writers in love. I wrote to him to suggest meeting and included Kim's phone number. He called, and Kim, Nancy, and I drove to Sommières, a lovely historic village near Montpellier.

"Call me Larry," he said when he met us outside his house. At seventy-six with a twinkle in his eye, he was totally charming. He smiled and invited us into his country home.

"That's a drawing Henry Miller's wife made of us in a café," Mr. Durrell said as I stopped to look at a wall dominated by photographs.

"Come on into the kitchen, and we'll have some drinks."

When I told him I no longer drank, he seemed offended.

"It's only wine then," he pouted as he put the brandy away. We talked about his *Alexandria Quartet*, France, politics, and bullfighting. I told him how much his writing had been an influence on me and showed him pictures of my kids.

He seemed intrigued about Scott being a gay drag performer and went to the hall, grabbed the famous photo of he and Henry Miller in bed together.

"Let me tell you the story of this. You must promise to never tell it to anyone." His laughter was restrained due to the emphysema that killed him the following year. He told us the story, but sadly, I've forgotten it.

Larry entertained us with a smooth charm—three strangers, as though we were family. He often asked about Susan, one of the loves of his life. He knew she was dying of AIDS.

"Visit me on your way back," Mr. Durrell whispered to me with a twinkle in his eye as I was getting in the car.

"I'll try," I said. The next day we left for Barcelona. I regret not having gone back.

* * *

My dreams would not let go of Lewis. In one, he proposed, in another he was in a wheel chair. I wrote a poem:

> One hour a day I think of you. One hour a day or more. One hour a day at least, I think of you and want you more. Each hour I hope you call...this hour, this day... One hour someday... When you call, I'll say I want you, please come and be with me, and if not, I will think of you each day, an hour each day or more.

Despite my determination to rid myself of the obsession with Lewis, I failed. His sweet lies of love mesmerized me as his promises kept me addicted.

In Barcelona, while the girls were out touring I found myself writing an endless letter to him. In Valencia I wrote, *Lewis, I know you are capable of changing, but I cannot help you except to say that alcoholism is only treatable by abstinence, and while you're heading for a bottom, I'm working on a recovery.*

In Madrid: *The past five months you've been disconnected and indifferent. The only time you seem to want me is when I've decided to stop seeing you.*

In Cordoba: *Get honest with yourself, you've done it before—even if your drinking is just the tip of the iceberg, remember how the Titanic was destroyed.* The letter was a half-attempted breakup with a plea to give it one last effort. I was still dancing backward like a contrary clown.

Carnaval was celebrated at the end of February while we were in Tarifa, the southernmost part of Spain. The girls and I were staying in a B&B where our host's three sons dressed up as ballerinas. They brought us to a party that Scott would have loved. It seemed most men dressed in drag and took it very seriously. I took dozens of pictures while wishing Scott were with us.

Castles all around—and I was telling myself fairytales. All the while reading *The Cinderella Complex*, by Collette Dowling. Lewis told me he'd been married to her. I believed him.

I sent the letter to Lewis from Portugal. Weeks later I arrived in New York, and there it was waiting for me. It was unopened, stuck in another envelope addressed to me with a note inside, "I would rather hear from you in person. Call me." I did call and pretended that I had not received it.

"Did you get my letter?" I asked after a short greeting.

"Ah, yes, but I, ah, sent it back to you. Ah, didn't you get it?"

"What do you mean, sent it back?" I kept up the façade, wanting him to explain why he hadn't opened the letter. He mumbled and stumbled awhile before I knew it was over.

That was it. I was done, my love addiction was broken. I swore never again to allow myself to be manipulated in an unhealthy relationship. *Thank you, God, I don't need any more men.* Or so I thought. My kids just laughed.

* * *

A few months later, while in Minneapolis I dreamt of a tall, thin, handsome, dark-haired man standing at the end of a long, empty table. The next day I called Kim and Jennifer on their birthdays. It was the Summer Solstice of 1989, and Jennifer invited me to her party that night.

"Sorry, I have to be in the darkroom all evening. My gallery opening is tomorrow and I still have photos to print for the show," I said.

"There's someone here I want you to meet." Jennifer persisted.

"All right, I'll come, but just for one hour, no more." I walked into her house and saw the man from my dream standing at the end of her dining room table. We locked eyes.

"My dear, sweet Pat, this is David Ekroth," she introduced. "He's an architect friend of Peter's." Peter was her husband.

The next thing I remembered was after my gallery opening. David and I were sitting at an outdoor café holding hands, enraptured with each other. We were together continuously for three more days in Minneapolis and until my plane took off to New York. I cried at the airport.

"Follow your heart," Scott advised me.

I had finally found the right man, even though he lived in Texas and I was in New York. No longer deluded, I trusted myself enough to know this time could possibly work out.

Misty and Jimmy Paulette in a Taxi, NYC,
1991, Photo by Nan Goldin

CHAPTER TWENTY-SIX

EAST VILLAGE DRAG

Linda Simpson, also from Minneapolis and a friend of Scott's, was living in New York in the late eighties and took thousands of photographs of her friends who dressed up. She said Misty, a.k.a. Miss Demeanor, was an art-world icon after being captured in one of photographer Nan Goldin's most famous and favorite photos: Misty and Jimmy Paulette in a Taxi, NYC. The photo, from 1991, was shot during the day, an unusual time for drag-queen starlets to be dolled up in wigs and heavy makeup. A few years later, it was published in Goldin's notable book *The Other Side*, featuring a slew of edgy gender-benders. Nan's fame had grown beyond the photography world since taking pictures of her drag friends in 1972 Boston. Her photographs and color slide/sound exhibits have been shown and collected internationally.

Misty and Jimmy were on their way to meet Linda and another drag queen, Lady Bunny, who'd invited them to hop aboard their ragtag float for the LGBT Pride Parade. Being creatures of the night, they made a monumental effort to schlep uptown before noon. Misty and Jimmy Paulette look serene in their photo, but they were probably half asleep.

The rest of the day was spent joyously cruising down Fifth Avenue on a flatbed truck. "Legalize Prostitution" was the theme—a great excuse for them to dress as sluts while delivering a vital message of sexual liberation. When the float finally got to

Christopher Street, it started pouring rain. Fatigued, they started laughing hysterically.

Linda took pictures that day, adding many to her collection, *The Drag Explosion*. Bunny, Tabboo!, Jimmy Paulette, Misty, and Linda were all part of the gang. In the late eighties and early nineties, they were part of the East Village's lively drag scene, which included performing at the punky, post-modern Pyramid Club. Misty posed for the cover of Linda's underground magazine, *My Comrade*. Scott's look in drag was rock-star sleek, tight latex and short punky wigs. On the flip side, her personality was laid back, a quiet queen surrounded by loudmouths. Miss Demeanor's calmness gave her an air of mystery. Scott did the makeup for Linda a few times. She said she'd never looked better.

In her magazine *My Comrade*, Linda's letter from the editor read:

> Years from now eager young homosexuals will ask us to reminisce about "the good old days"—The Gay 90s.
>
> We'll smile as we stroll down memory lane remembering all the crazy dances and freaky fashions, the wacky hairstyles and goofy music, the drag superstars, Madonna, and MTV.
>
> Most importantly we'll recall how brave we were, and how we mobilized against great adversity with boundless enthusiasm, and proved that the will of good people is so much stronger than the sinister and corrupt.
>
> Rightfully we could have been bitter, living in a society that did its best to squash us. Instead, we were a joyous, loving sort who greeted each other warmly with hugs and kisses.
>
> We'll tell our rapt listeners that regretfully we didn't get to hear much about our own history. Because in the past straight society sucked up gay people's talents and skills, yet refused to grant their wholeness as lesbians and gays. In the 90s we put an end to that nonsense.

EAST VILLAGE DRAG

We'll look back at the 90s as a ground-breaking decade when gay people were heroes and freedom fighters who paved the way for the gay 2000s. It was the 90s when we created a gay past as well as a future.

After staying in a series of crash pads in the rough-and-tumble East Village, Scott rented an apartment above a Catholic Church with two other drag roommates. Linda thought it was a fab idea for a sitcom—Holy Rollers below, sinners above.

* * *

Scott's life took a turn in 1995 when he moved in with his boyfriend. He also had started his makeup career and didn't have time for drag. Feelings were hurt, but Linda understood. Which one of them hadn't fantasized about abandoning their bohemian lives for more luxurious surroundings? Over the next couple of decades, Scott's occasional encounters with Linda were amiable. She still found him down-to-earth and sweet. And more than once, Scott mentioned he was eager to do another whirl as Misty.

In the fall of 2013, Scott and Linda began socializing again after many years. The relationship with his long-term boyfriend had ended. They had lived together for eighteen years. When it was over, Scott reached out to members of his old crowd. He entered phase-two of his friendship with Linda, as both were more mature and insightful adults, but they were still silly with each other.

It was an early beautiful summer day in June, 2014 when Scott emailed Linda to cancel a plan to get together.

"I apologize for being squirrely." It was one of his last emails.

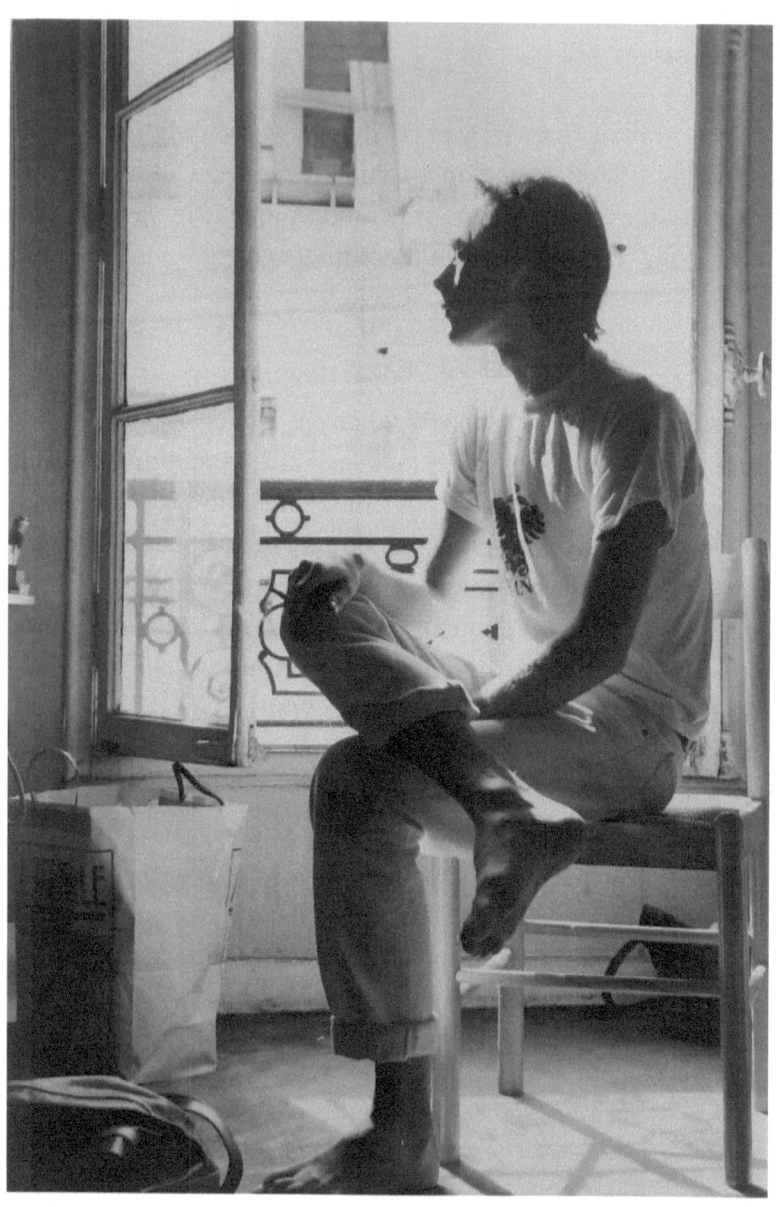

Scott in Paris, 1991, PA

CHAPTER TWENTY-SEVEN

PARIS

In 1989, shortly after I met and fell in love with David Ekroth, he invited me to visit him in Italy in the fall. I flew to Rome, and after a few days on Elba, we drove to a castle in Castiglion Fiorentino in Tuscany, Italy. He was there to teach architecture for three months to third-year and grad students from the program at Texas A&M University. After the term ended, we traveled through Germany and France before we broke up briefly in early 1990.

My mother passed away, leaving me a few thousand dollars. I took it as my chance to finally go where my soul had longed for during the painful twenty years of motherhood—Paris. I sensed I'd suffered a PTSD-like reaction, as if I'd been held hostage by kids and addictions.

Unfortunately, I didn't know how to parent until years after Scott and Kim had left the nest and I had stopped drinking. Kim was in college in Minneapolis and Scott was living his dream on the lower East Side of New York City, settling into place with like-minded friends and colleagues. Neither of them wanted parenting from me. I was sick of New York, relationships, and obligations.

My sister Nancy wrote in a card, "When are you going to get tired of running around the world, looking for something you have lots of here at home—people who really care about you? Happiness is not something you can find in a different place. It comes from within your heart and can happen anywhere, if you give it a chance and work at it."

Yes, good advice. But I was grieving my mother's death and wanted to run away.

I moved to Paris knowing no one there, having no job, hoping to find a gallery and make art.

My mother had never liked my being so far away. "But Paris is across the *ocean*," she'd say.

I justified the move when I got the money she'd left me. I wanted to celebrate my recovery from all dependencies, believing Kim or Scott no longer needed me.

Through my instant family of strangers in AA and Al-Anon, I found a couch to stay on, a job teaching English, and a supportive network. Twelve-step programs were filled with generous men and women looking for new sober friends. The out-patient treatment I'd attended a few years before and a group called Women for Sobriety had saved me, and I found support I didn't have or couldn't see before I'd given up drugs.

Living in Paris also became an opportunity for Scott to accept drag jobs and makeup assignments there. I found a sublet in the center of Paris near the Chatelet metro station and arranged for Scott to come visit. Both sober now, we bonded in a new way, engaging and enjoying each other's creative sides. The special relationship I had with Scott was partly due to our artistic temperaments and addictions. We were happy to be together again.

Scott booked a gig doing makeup and invited me to the Petite Palais backstage to watch him turn young women into gorgeous creatures for a fashion show. Skinny, average-looking girls of eighteen and nineteen were transitioned into even more glamorous, exquisite women after leaving Scott's chair. The models loved him joking and speaking French to them. Scott had taught himself French in high school, and he loved Paris as much as I did. We took to the people, language, and lifestyle as if we were *born* French. He even began to look French.

The window in our apartment overlooked rue St. Denis, where

older prostitutes leaned against doorways, usually smoking a cigarette while waiting for customers. Scott befriended one, easily in her sixties (yet looking seventy) who smiled up at him each morning. He brought her a croissant one day and I watched them chat, from the window.

"I made a new friend today," he later told me.

Scott had great understanding of and compassion for women in the oldest profession. It started when he met several prostitutes in jail after his car accident in 1979, when he was fifteen. In the early eighties, I took Scott to Coyote meetings. "Call Off Your Old Tired Ethics" was a prostitute's rights organization held at my friend Flo Kennedy's home and office in midtown Manhattan. Flo, Margo St. James, and other women fought for prostitutes' rights and the decriminalization of the profession. Flo believed prostitutes did not *sell* their bodies, they simply *rented* them.

"It's housewives who *sell* their bodies," she said.

Years later, in drag, Scott joined sex workers on their floats during the LGBT parades in lower Manhattan. He loved all the disenfranchised, unconditionally and without judgement. In Paris, as we looked out the window at the prostitutes, we spoke of our shared respect for them, as the French had. It was summer, and we were enjoying our favorite city.

When Scott left Paris after a few weeks, I became lonely and confused. It was a warm, sunny day when I sat sobbing on a bench at St. Catherine's Square in the Marais. My son was back in New York, my mother was gone, and I had broken up with David again. He'd been the best relationship I'd ever found—creative, gentle, sensible, patient, and understanding of my moods and stubbornness. I couldn't bear the loss.

"Why am I so sad?" I wondered. Here I was, living in my preferred city and doing my art. I even arranged for an exhibit of my recent work in a good gallery near the Marais. The well-known dealer Antoine Candau had opened a large new space and would include my collages in his next show of Robert Rauschenberg's work. I was honored but scared to exhibit with such a famous, well-loved artist.

Fear turned into panic. Would I need to find a paid job? Could I support myself by selling my art? Could I support Scott if he asked to live with me in Paris? I had lived with concern for his sobriety for two years since he finished drug treatment at the hospital in Minnesota. These questions and doubts fed my tears.

The dark corner in my mind where my own and my son's ability to stay off drugs or alcohol was another awful unknown. I would need to be strong.

Misdemeanor (Misty) in Berlin with unknown friend and me, 1992, PA, UNI and David Ekroth

CHAPTER TWENTY-EIGHT

BERLIN AND FAME

Nan Goldin photographed the drag scene on the streets of New York before and after Scott began performing. Misty became a star as much through these photographs in her book, *The Other Side*, as from the shows.

"I used to think that I could never lose anyone if I photographed them enough. In fact, my pictures show me how much I've lost," Nan said.

She wrote that drag queens were "truly revolutionary, winning the battle of the sexes because they have stepped out of the ring." While both Scott and Nan were living in Berlin in the early nineties, Scott performed as Misty in Paris, Berlin, and London before returning to New York for his expanding career as a makeup artist.

By 1989, East Berlin had become a squatter's paradise for artists, dissidents, punks, rockers, transvestites, and drag queens. A few years later, Scott was squatting with his friend Ilya in a huge apartment on Oranien Strasse in the center of the Kreuzberg district.

David visited me in Paris and we drove to Berlin. After reuniting our on-again-off-again long-distance relationship, we'd spent months together in Houston before I moved back to Paris. I had tried to warm up to Texas but could not tolerate the good-old-boy gun environment. Another split. We traveled well together but couldn't agree to where we should live. I needed Paris or New

York, and he was not ready to give up teaching architecture or his tenured position at Texas A&M.

When we arrived in Berlin, we were amazed at the enormous, gymnasium-sized space Scott and Ilya had found.

"How many people live here?" I guessed maybe ten or more by the number of rooms.

"Just Ilya and I," Scott answered. "There are hundreds of these buildings, abandoned by the GDR [German Democratic Republic] after the wall fell. Take any room you like." We decided on the one Scott had put a blow-up mattress in.

Located among desolate streets lined with gray, bullet-holed, rundown World War II buildings, I wondered if it would be safe for us to walk the neighborhood.

"It just *looks* dangerous," Scott assured me. "But it's really very safe,"

I figured if he had managed to live in Alphabet City, the lower East Side of Manhattan, for two years, he *would* think this lawless, transient area was safe.

Though David and I did not stay long enough to attend the show, Scott invited me to a rehearsal in one of the spontaneous, word-of-mouth weekend clubs where he would be performing. He dressed in half drag wearing a curly bright-red wig, black bustier, full makeup, and high boots for our walk the eleven blocks to the club. Scott usually wore rolled-up blue jeans and a black jacket as "street" wear, which I assumed was for the elders on the street.

As we passed many young people, several boys greeted Scott with salutations, "Hallo, Tag," and other friendly comments and slang that I suspected referred to his makeup and high heels. Judging by his smile, I knew my son was in the right place.

Scott had studied German from age ten, and it was finally paying off. I listened to his articulate instructions with the stage manager, lighting engineer, and sound man—and watched the way he strutted back and forth on the stage speaking in German and lip-syncing in English with an impressive, commanding presence.

BERLIN AND FAME

David picked us up at the stage door and took a photograph of Scott and me. I wore a large purple shirt over short black skirt and tights. Scott held a large black bag, his arm around my shoulder and mine around his waist.

I later found the photo and a clipping from his papers, which were in his apartment along with drag-show invitations and a box of pictures of himself and friends, many dressed as glamorous women:

> Miss Demeanor *Fehlverhalten* [in German]–is a spunky yet serious-minded Sagittarian from New York. Her interests are fashion and early French philosophy. Her measurements are: 36-22-36. Although she lives in New York, she has chosen Berlin as her "home-away-from-home" and is currently dividing her time between difficult philosophical theories and making occasional social appearances and performances.... A bit shy, she loves to socialize and quickly warms up to strangers. So don't let her arrogant "stand-offish" attitude keep you away–it's just one of her many defense mechanisms.

These words were typed, cut and pasted onto two pages with color copies and Polaroid photos of Scott in drag. Perhaps it was a mock-up for a 1992 German magazine from the time Scott lived in Berlin.

The writer Oscar Wilde said, "You are who you pretend to be." I wonder if, by pretending on so many occasions to be a woman, he became the sensitive, elegant man who charmed most everyone he met. He looked deep into their eyes with his endearing smile, the same smile he'd had since birth–authentic and unpretentious.

When performing, he wore a bright light-blue, violet, blond, red, or black wig that was short, spikey, long, straight, or curly. Scott chose carefully when designing his outfits and makeup to enhance a different thing, a total "look" he was after. Shopping in thrift stores or vintage shops and occasionally picking up designer items from the makeup jobs he worked on, Scott searched for glitter, sequins, big hair, and high-heeled shoes. He enhanced them with the right jewelry, usually showy and large, including hoop earrings, rhinestone-covered dog collars, dangly stone necklaces and oversized flashy rings worn naturally on manicured hands. And, of course, perfect makeup.

As Misty danced across the stage, she paused at times to demurely pose for pictures before, during, and after the show or while meeting her many admirers. I was as proud of my son then as when he'd been a child, but now I was with a group of appreciators who delighted in the performance of a man dressed as a woman. Misty was no longer my son at these shows. She was a made-up character showing off her talents. I often called and invited friends to see a Misty drag show, to join me in watching the flawless characterization of Scott transformed into a woman. It felt familiar to me.

In the photos from Scott's and my collections and Nan's books, there are several dozen different "looks" of Miss Demeanor or Misty: sultry, flamboyant, all carefully orchestrated and executed. An invite welcoming Miss Demeanor back to New York from Berlin shows a photo of Scott in full makeup and wig, announcing Afro-Dite as guest host. I imagine Lady Bunny, Linda Simpson, Kabuki, and Ru Paul were there along with Scott's many other friends.

I was still living in Paris and regretted having missed that show.

The costumes are mostly gone now, or given away. A few items I cannot part with, like the sequined sleeveless top and silk yellow jacket that I wore once on New Year's Eve.

The makeup is still in several cases, and his life mask resides in a box on the work table in my studio after having been photographed—the images to be used in my art. Am I trying to bring him back to life? In my journal, yes. Certainly, when he speaks to me he is still alive. I have him in my dreams and the artwork, photos, and sculpture. Perhaps his things and my memories will inspire something tangible for others to see.

CHAPTER TWENTY-NINE

PROFESSIONAL BEGINNINGS

Scott returned from Berlin to New York in late 1992. Vincent Mallardi, owner of Alcone—a makeup distributor in Long Island City—hired him to manage his Chelsea store.

In an article in *Allure Magazine*, Mallardi said, "Scott's fascination was not just with the application of makeup, but the product itself. Before we opened the store in Manhattan, he would hang out for hours in our Long Island City factory. He became part of the family. We'd leave him alone, and he'd examine every product, every color, experimenting endlessly. Scott was a big reason the store happened because we both knew he could manage it. Alcon took off, in part due to Scott Andrew, who ran it like it was his own."

"I pushed Vinny to open the store," Scott said. He loved Alcon and made it feel like an old-time apothecary. Scott met makeup artists and started booking jobs for himself, often working in return for clothing samples or magazine tear sheets for his portfolio. He began to build his career as *Scott Andrew*, using only his first and middle names.

I remembered the many times Scott intensely watched me put on my makeup before going out and how—from an early age—he stared at every brush, eyeshadow, rouge, and applicator as he studied the changes in my face. All the actors wore makeup in his shows, and by age eight, the dressing room Scott created in our basement held a full vanity with makeup, jewelry, and wigs that any drag queen would be giddy over.

Scott had learned about shading, mixing colors, and compositional balance from his studies at the Children's Theater of the Art Institute and the Minneapolis College of Art and Design. He parlayed this knowledge with his experience from years of doing his own and other performers' makeup at drag shows. His career took off. Scott was hired to do makeup for the B-52s, Bobby Brown, and Boys II Men music videos, and Nan Goldin recommended he be hired for a movie-set job in Berlin.

***

In September, 1994, late summer leaves gently danced across the long, red carpet leading up to the tent at Bryant Park. Scott had asked me to visit him during New York Fashion Week, where he would be doing the makeup for models in a show for a designer everyone there seemed to know except me. Years later, after hours of research I still wasn't able to find the designer's name.

The large tent had a section partitioned off barely wide enough to hold twenty or more small tables with chairs, half of which were occupied by models. Makeup artists were bent over as they enhanced eyes with pencils, mascara, and shadow; cheeks with blush; and lips with liner and color on the women, most of whom appeared to be teenagers.

When Scott saw me, he waved and secretly motioned me over and introduced me to the model he was attending. Her face was unremarkable. When she stood up, I realized this six-foot-tall, very thin, small breasted model with a blank expression in her eyes was, essentially, a mannequin to make designer clothes look good. I knew my son would turn her into a ravishing beauty.

A noisy chaos buzzed around me as artists, half-clothed models in curlers, and a Japanese film crew were coming and going, asking Scott for instructions. Other makeup artists, a cameraman, an audio guy, and an interviewer asked and received brief advice, and I could see that Scott was in charge. The film crew was there to record his application style, and the twenty makeup artists were being directed by him. He was clearly the boss. I was impressed and secretly relieved that he no longer needed to borrow money from me.

I squeezed into a twenty-square-inch space by the mirror to watch my son create his magic. Looking deeply at the model's face, Scott saw the glow from within that only an artist could see. It was as if he stopped thinking, sinking into silent motion. In less than twenty minutes, when time seemed to stand still, Scott transformed an ordinary woman into an exquisite goddess that made me gasp. She herself, when looking in the mirror, appeared to see an image of herself as a culmination of all the famous models she had worshipped.

The writer Colette said, "There is nothing that gives more assurance than a mask." The plain girl sitting in the chair that day was gone. Her new-found beauty and self-esteem emboldened her. She stood erect and confident.

"It's amazing how little time you needed to make such beauty!" I whispered to my son.

Five years after Scott's passing, I found a photo from that day. His face glances at me as he smiles in the photo, dressed in a red and blue flowered shirt over an olive-green tee. Perhaps that shirt was from the designer, since he often received partial pay in clothing. It was his habit to give me many of those items. I treasure the Helmut Lang tuxedo pants, though it is unlikely I will ever fit into them again. The large-shouldered, Sylvia Heisel suit still hangs in my closet with other treasures long out of style.

From 1994 to 2012, Scott's career shot to the top. He made $5,000/day or more as makeup artist on photo shoots, while his models graced the covers of *Vogue, Elle, Allure, Flair, Vanity Fair, Rolling Stone*, etc. His career expanded as celebrities were given new faces and personas by the famous Scott Andrew. Liza

Minelli, Annette Benning, Claire Danes, Julianne Moore, Hilary Swank, Jennifer Connelly, Sarah Jessica Parker, and hundreds of other supermodels and actresses all turned their faces to his careful, deft hand. Many became friends.

Scott with Liza Minnelli and Ru Paul and as Misdemeanor, NYC, c. 1996 – 2002, UNI

CHAPTER THIRTY

MEETING JED

My partner David Ekroth and I had just moved into our house in Woodstock, New York in late spring, 1995. After six years of living in different places, we had finally committed to a long-term relationship, enough to buy a house together. David continued teaching architecture in Texas and came up summers, spring, fall and winter breaks to work on the additions and construction needed for the house. I was selling advertising part-time at the *Woodstock Times* and working on my collage art.

Scott first brought Jed Root to our house in the summer of 1995. I had heard about him many times since he and Scott were friends who'd met in New York in the late eighties. They went on trips together to exotic locations such as Cambodia and Thailand, first as friends, or at least, not as *exclusive* boyfriends. I knew they were lovers but respected Scott's saying "friend" or "boyfriend."

"Jed wants me to go to Vietnam, but I can't afford it," Scott had told me months before. He had just started his career as a makeup artist and was paid in trade and little cash. I had given him loans when I could, but I wasn't about to help pay for his trip with a wealthy lover.

"Why don't you ask him to pay your expenses? If he wants you to go with him and you can't afford it, he should pay," I suggested.

"I'll think about it," Scott said. Jed was a successful representative of makeup artists, hairdressers, and fashion photographers, and clearly could afford to pay for Scott.

Our new home in Willow, a hamlet of Woodstock, was a small ranch house set near a creek in the Catskill Mountains that needed a lot of work, including a paint job.

"I can hire you to paint the house. That'll help with your trip, but I still think you need to speak to Jed about money," I advised Scott before he brought Jed up for a visit, remembering what it was like to have a rich friend who'd wanted me to travel with her. A friend and a lover are different though. I understood his wanting to pay his own way.

At that time the kitchen in the house was only six-by-six feet, and included a bar with stools. I struggled over the old stove, attempting to boil water in a new, too-large pot. The pot held four times the amount of water needed for the pasta I was making. Knowing Scott had bragged about my cooking, I was a bit nervous. They arrived on time. Jed was handsome with long, dark hair, moustache, and carefully trimmed underlip and chin beards, a shorter version of Johnny Depp. He initiated no conversation as he sat at our tiny kitchen bar, an arm's length away from me, hand under his chin, staring at my back as I cooked. Thinking he might be shy, I attempted to open a conversation by asking questions and making a few comments, hoping to spark a dialogue.

"I think I put too much water in the pot," I said. Silence. Hmmm. "I'm afraid dinner will be a bit delayed."

"Dump some water out," he directed me.

"Well, that's a good idea," I said, wondering if I had given him the impression that I was a novice cook, or worse yet, stupid. I turned to dump out half the water. Jed had his eyes on the sink and pot without looking up at my face. "He's shy," I thought.

Scott was in the living room slouched on an old hand-me-down sofa, looking at books I had brought home from the library. He was not going to help and seemed uncaring about his new boyfriend or me. I approached him.

"Scott, why don't you join us?" I asked as the smile drained off my face. I wanted to scream, "Help!"

"Okay—in a minute." Silence. I returned to the kitchenette and started to ask Jed questions.

"Where is your apartment in the city?"

"Chinatown."

"Is it far from your office?"

"No."

"Do you walk to work?"

"I take a taxi."

"I use to rep photographers in the city in the early eighties," I offered. No response.

"Do you know Ryuzo?"

"No."

"Benno Friedman?"

"No."

"How many people do you handle?"

"About thirty."

I paused as the water started to boil along with my patience.

Scott finally came in and sat on the other stool. "What's up?"

"Your mom is having trouble boiling water." Jed smiled at me.

I started to like him a bit but was wary of him at the same time. Sarcasm was something I allowed only from my family, and he was certainly not my family. I decided this boyfriend would not be around for long. I was wrong. Scott moved in with him the next month.

* * *

Scott and Jed had been living together for over a year when Jed called me, sounding frantic.

"*OH MY GOD!!! SCOTT'S IN JAIL!!* He jumped the turnstile in the subway, he was caught in a sting and the cops *arrested* him! Can you come to the city? He said his metro card didn't work and the line was too long to buy another card. He didn't have time to wait."

"Slow down," I said. "What do you want me to do?" Jed and I had gradually warmed up to each other since our first meeting.

"You could go to the station and plead with the cops. Tell them it was your fault, or that he is seriously ill, autistic. Hell, tell them he's insane and didn't know what he was doing. I don't know, say *anything*, but we can't leave him there. Do you *know* what they do to gays in the lower Manhattan jail? *WE'VE GOT TO GET HIM OUT!!!*"

"Calm down. Let's think this through. By the time I get there, it may be too late. It will take me three or more hours to drive a hundred miles on a Sunday night in August."

"What *can* we do?" Jed asked.

"Can you call a lawyer? Explain the situation and tell him he has to go there ASAP and not leave until Scott's freed."

Jed and his lawyer paid the $25,000 bail and Scott was released before morning. A few weeks later, when it was okay to joke about it, I asked Scott, "How did the night in jail downtown compare to the Long Island City jail?" I was referring back to the Forest Hills car crash and the prostitutes he met in jail that had so inspired him when he was fifteen.

"No comparison," Scott answered with a smile. "There *was* one consolation. I had a pimp for my cellmate and we discussed makeup."

CHAPTER THIRTY-ONE

RELATIONSHIPS

Scott was settled in Jed's Chinatown apartment. Jed had come from Louisiana to New York in 1982 with his makeup-artist friend, Kevyn Aucoin. Scott met them both at meetings for recovering drug addicts in the East Village. Jed had continued to represent Kevyn off and on as his career took off and even after they split.

As someone who had been a photographer's representative in the early eighties, when I heard that Jed did *not* want to represent Scott, I intervened, explaining it would be a mistake. Resentment or jealousy could occur while one watched the other rise to fame alone. Scott was starting a new career and Jed had risen to the top of the rep business. I believed his helping Scott would *not* be the recipe for disaster Jed worried about. Their relationship could and *would* only work if he represented Scott.

"You need to be partners in your careers as well." I pleaded. Jed agreed and became Scott's agent, and soon jobs and opportunities for Scott Andrew came more frequently.

In 2000, the South Korean AmorePacific cosmetics company hired Scott to design a full line of makeup for their relatively new brand, Laneige, named after the French word for *snow*. They chose Scott because he was an internationally known makeup artist and would steer the company forward as they expanded their market beyond China, Japan, and Korea into Europe and Russia. Scott had excelled at chemistry in school and enjoyed the research and development side of cosmetics. He had a thing for playing with the products, experimenting with mineral oil or canola oil. Twice a year, before traveling to Korea Scott would come to my studio to develop the master plan and create the color charts Laneige required.

"Should we be referring to the hundred-page report from their designers?" I asked.

"No, *I'm* the designer. That report is just theories from the trend experts that Laneige hires. What do they know?"

Scott continued to search images from drawers and stacks of old books and magazines I had saved for my mixed media collage artwork and classes. He wanted to find the right shade, the perfect texture, and the ideal *feel* of what *he* imagined for the next season's line. I assisted as best I could, a familiar pride welling up in me.

When Scott flew to Korea he was met at the Seoul airport by a screaming crowd of young women and girls holding a life-size cardboard image of Scott Andrew. He seemed to be the newest fashion icon. Laneige gained in sales each year, and the contract was renewed for eight years. When I asked Scott why it ended, he shrugged and looked up to the sky as if the answer was there, waiting.

"Who knows?"

Months later, I read a review in the *Musings of a Muse* online magazine about the 2008 Laneige collection. A press agent had written, "As always, the promo model image is gorgeous! It's a very edgy look they created using soft colors." I knew that in the fashion and makeup business, there is little loyalty, only fads, smoke and mirrors.

In 2000, the same year he began with Laneige, Scott did Hilary Swank's makeup at the Academy Awards show. She had won the best actress award for *Boys Don't Cry* and Scott was so proud he called me from LA that evening.

"I'm in Hilary's room, she just came in and tossed the award on the sofa, saying I can share it with her!" He sounded as if he had touched the sky.

Another honored moment he shared—there were only a few, as he rarely boasted—was a phone call on my birthday saying his friend wanted to wish me a Happy Birthday. He paused and I waited.

"Happy Birthday, Scott's mom." His friend said. We had a pleasant conversation about the party and Scott. Within minutes, I heard Scott laughing in the background. Then he took the phone and asked me whom I thought was talking to me.

"I don't know, but your friend sounds nice, is she a model?" I asked. Scott laughed.

"Mom. That was *LIZA MINELLI!*"

He also related an encounter with Sarah Jessica Parker, our favorite from *Sex and The City*.

"*YOU'RE* Scott Andrew? I've been wanting to meet you for such a long time, to ask you to do my makeup!" she exclaimed when they first met. Admiring his previous work, she begged him to do her makeup for the MTV movie awards she would host.

"I wanted to toughen up her girl-next-door sweetness with strong, sultry eyes," Scott was quoted in a 2004 *Allure* magazine makeup interview—though he usually wanted a natural look for his clients.

Numerous editorial articles on his rise as a makeup artist followed. Scott was the star of three videos on makeup lessons for a fashion company on YouTube. Other top jobs and countless magazine covers (Scott did over one hundred for *Allure* alone), fashion stories, events, ads, and award shows came frequently as his career advanced.

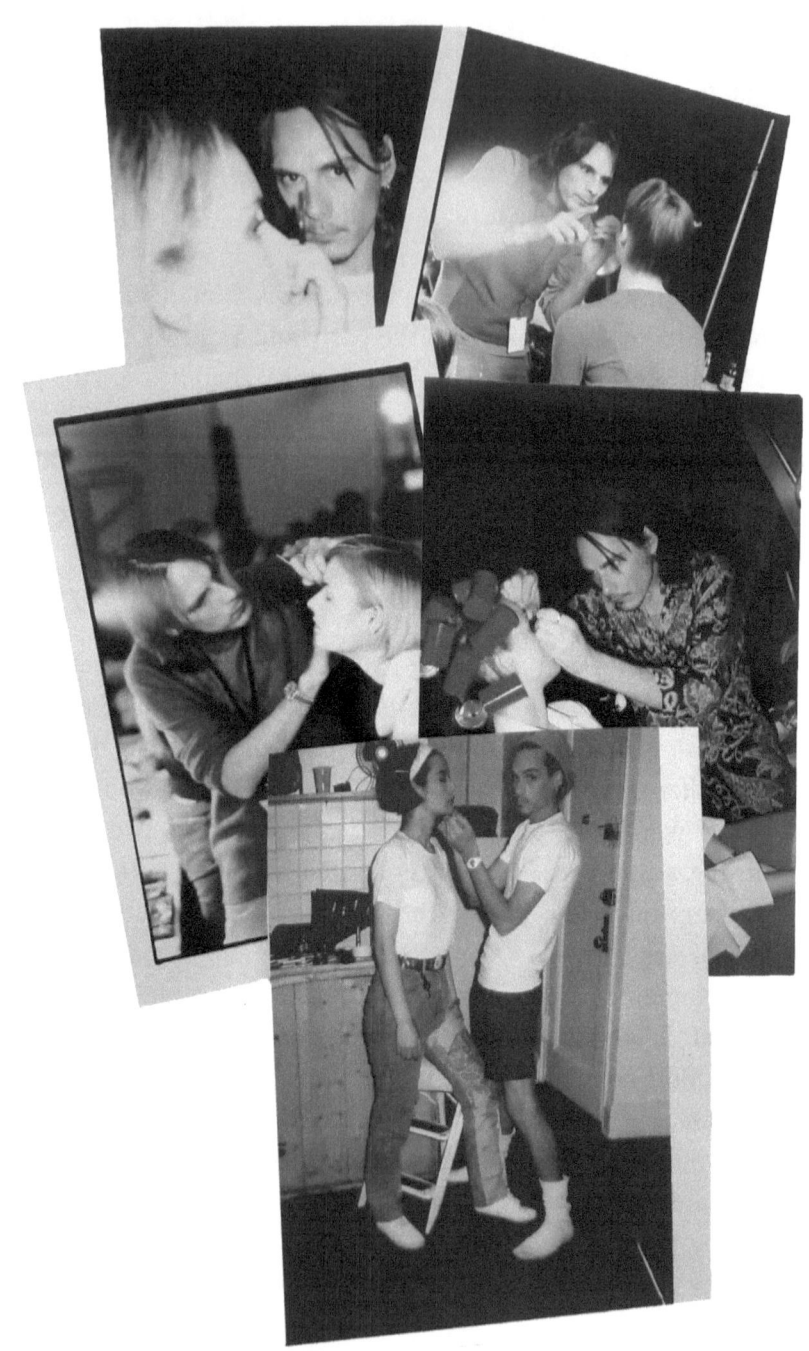

Scott doing makeup on unknown models,
NYC, c. 1994 – '99, PA and UNI

CHAPTER THIRTY-TWO

KEVYN AND TECHNIQUE

By 1995 Scott was making a name for himself, while Kevyn Aucoin was the top makeup artist in the world. He became both a friend and a mentor to Scott. They would sit together on the steps at Alcone in Long Island City for hours discussing makeup, the fashion business, and other shared interests. Somehow, the two stayed friends, despite Kevyn's past relationship with Jed. Kevyn respected both Scott's and Jed's talents and wanted to help whenever possible.

David and I were invited to Kevyn's country home in upstate New York. The beautiful estate had been previously owned by Laura Ashley. We hoped to get ideas for our new home in Willow. Kevyn showed us around the property and house, pointing out the changes he had made. I was astounded by his energy and we formed an immediate friendship. Sadly, it would be a brief one, though. On 9/11, as the Twin Towers were disintegrating, Kevyn was diagnosed with a brain tumor. Six months after having surgery, he passed away unexpectedly in May 2002. He was only forty.

"I work in an industry with some of the meanest people who have ever walked the face of the earth, who live and die for the surface. But the way I see it, I have a responsibility to do the most I can do, the way I know how. Since I know how to apply makeup, that's what I do and use it as a platform. Glamour is not cruelty.

Glamour is not closed-mindedness. Glamour is not bigotry or hatred. Glamour is not self-centeredness. Glamour, most of all, is not self-conscious; it's not trying really hard. It's just expressing your own truth. I think that's what the essence of glamour really is—expressing your uniqueness," Kevyn said.

Hilary Swank loved Kevyn. "We were very, very close," she said in an interview in one magazine. Jed loved Kevyn. They had lived together for more than ten years. And Scott loved Hilary, Kevyn, and Jed. They were as close as relationships got in the fashion world.

* * *

When searching the tear sheets for Scott's few words amongst the thousands of faces he'd made up, I came across proof sheets with his handwritten notations, marking corrections needed: "Too strong—lighten—shadows too dark—lessen—soften—restore original—remove."

In other magazines quoting Scott, I found more clues to his technique: "Natural no longer means appearing as though you're not wearing anything at all, just limit yourself to a single sensational element.... It's lips, lids or lashes, never all 3 at once." He suggested playing (cautiously) with metallic "A dab of bronzy blush never hurt." Scott liked the glam-rock look inspired by David Bowie, and at least once used it for a print job.

"I added a silver, dripping slash on his cheeks and some black eye makeup." He told the writer from *W Magazine*.

In another interview he said, "Julianne Moore is a natural beauty and Claire Danes is young and beautiful, but everyone needs a *little* concealer." Other magazines tell more of his advice, "A 'satin' texture is a step down from dewy but a step up from 'matte.' If your skin is dry, rub a tiny dot of Vaseline over each cheekbone.... Too much foundation looks unnatural. Sometimes my job is about deciding what to leave undone." I searched further. In his personal papers, I found Scott's theories in his own handwriting:

> My Philosophy of Makeup is based on my love for the infinite uniqueness of nature. I find beauty everywhere in the natural world and obtain much inspiration from it. Flowers, birds, leaves, etc. I'm an avid orchid gardener—and to me this is just another extension of what I do—nurture and create the environment for beauty to express itself. Our society judged beauty by certain standards of similarity. I oppose this idea. Everyone is unique and it is our differences that make us interesting. Change is naturally uncomfortable for most people, but the fashion and beauty industry are driven by it.

The above was crossed out with a big X—and on the other side, again in his own handwriting:

> Makeup is an art. Cosmetology, a science. Any art requires knowledge and skill, which come from years of study and practice. Being a makeup artist involves knowledge of light and shadow, color theory, form and structure, and painting technique. It requires an eye for detail and obsession with perfection.
>
> All of this can be very intimidating to a woman who merely wants to appear well-groomed or wishes to attempt a little creative self-expression.
>
> I hope to dispel this fear many women have by encouraging education through experimentation with a policy of "anything goes," There are no rules in makeup. Each woman must ultimately decide for herself what type of makeup suits her best. The world around us is constantly changing—and so too is the way we perceive beauty. In the past beauty was judged by rigid standards. In our uniqueness it is our differences that make us interesting.

LOVING SCOTT

> In my work I strive to offer new possibilities—or new ways of looking at existing ideas, always attempting to stretch the limits and expand our definition of beauty.

I don't know why the first page was crossed out. I actually prefer his ideas about nature providing inspiration. Someone who saw or heard the first draft must have proposed the changes. I suspected these pages may have been done for his Laneige contract one year and wonder if any of the millions who have seen Scott Andrew's "art" will sense the mystery and poetry of his interior life, which broke loose, radiated, and communicated itself in all of his creations.

Magazine pages with Liza and others, NYC, c. 1996 – 2010, Michael Thompson and UNI

CHAPTER THIRTY-THREE

A MEMORY

Wet cobblestones glistened from a recent rain as we left the New York Soho restaurant where we celebrated my missed birthday. The previous week, Scott had been in Minneapolis for his father's birthday and to introduce Jed to family and friends. I asked them both how it went.

Jed blurted out, "Well, Scott gave his father a five-hundred-dollar-bottle of Merlot as a gift."

I stopped dead in the middle of the street while the words cut into my abdomen. I couldn't move. Hurt, anger, sadness, and jealousy expanded from inside my whole body. Trembling with a sense of injustice from the years of his father's not sending Scott cards or calling, no gifts or financial support to his only son—and then Scott gives him a $500-bottle of French wine?

Scott defended the gift. "I just gave him a birthday present to thank him for hosting us," he stated calmly, while continuing to cross the street. A slight smile on his face gave me the impression of some embarrassment or guilt in his excuse.

"You barely give me cards for my birthday or Mother's Day! Who raised you? Who went to court to get your college fund freed up? Who supported you in the shows you put on and performed in. Who supplied the makeup, wigs, or the prom dresses?" Filled with self-pity, I kept the rant going for another block.

Painful memories of the years raising my children poured in. I remembered times before the separation when Scott's father was around but not really *there*. Always working in the garage on his cars, boats, or motorcycles in his free time, begrudging the kids or me anything for ourselves or the house. He was late to every party, event, concert, and movie while laboring away on some engine, an engine clearly more important to him than his children. This was also the father who went to work, came home, criticized or ignored us, and often fell asleep on the sofa.

"I'm sorry you feel that way," Scott said. I couldn't believe he had forgotten the unfairness and abuse of his childhood, or seeing my distress.

I shuddered with my grievances about the past as I saw my son look up to a clear sky. The stars he'd so loved since he was seven were sparkling brighter and stronger than usual. Was he remembering those nights we stayed up late to view them?

"*I'm* sorry it makes me so angry," I whispered.

We spent the following moments in silence before reaching their loft on lower Broadway, where I would be spending the night.

I began to understand that Scott wanted to buy his father's love and was curious how Jed felt about the gift. He didn't even want to go to Minneapolis and clearly understood my disapproval. The risk he had taken making Scott angry by tattling seemed worth it. Scott looked contrite while Jed had a satisfied smile on his face.

"Want some cake?" Jed asked as we passed a bakery still open. My resentment remained, but I never spoke of it again.

A few weeks later I received a box with a beautiful string of blue pearls from Scott. "A belated birthday present," his note told me. Though I've never had them appraised, I'm certain they cost more than $500. I felt justified.

CHAPTER THIRTY-FOUR

THE CASTLE

At the high end of White's Road in Palenville, NY, on the edge of the Catskill Mountains with an expansive view of the Berkshires and the Hudson River, sits a 1917 mansion surrounded by a guest house, the Vista house, and a cottage. The townspeople call the big house the castle, though it is more like a manor house.

Jed bought the estate after he and Scott had rented a house for four years in Willow, close to where I live, ninety miles from New York City. They loved the area, and Scott wanted to be near me. At first they lived in the castle on weekends only. Later, Scott spent most of the week there, going into the city only for work a few days a week. It was their second home together, for fourteen years.

My son and I were there often, pruning the apricot, Japanese lilac, or peony trees in front. On September 11, 2001, Scott was in New York City. I was at home in Willow, in shock, watching the World Trade Center go down on TV. I remembered the time my mother, sister, and I saw planes flying below us as we dined in the restaurant on the top floor.

I thought of Scott and Jed's apartment, less than a mile north of the Trade Center. Scott was there getting ready for work and later told us he saw a plane fly low over their skylight. Jed was at his office below Canal Street, only blocks north of the Trade Center. I tried to call but the phone and cable lines were down. Lower Manhattan was in total chaos.

After watching the terrible images on TV for hours that morning, I was lured to the castle. I needed a way to feel closer to Scott. Since I had to water his orchids the next day anyway, I got in the car and drove the twenty-five-minute trip to the castle in a daze.

Driving through the stone-covered gatehouse, past the sunken boxwood-maze garden and pool with trellis cover, I arrived at the classical front pillars and large lions guarding the huge double front doors. The house and grounds were peaceful, holding no element of strangeness or danger.

After entering through the vestibule, French doors opened onto a huge great-room with twenty-foot ceilings circled by balconies front and back. This was a home that stood removed from the twenty-first century. A library to the left was filled with thousands of books, many of which came from the Woodstock Library. I was volunteering for the Friends of the library, working in the book barn. They threw out hundreds of books each week, especially the older cloth- or leather-bounds no one wanted. Most were over eighty years old.

"Mom, could you get leather- or cloth-bound books there—" Scott asked after moving in— "preferably art, science, music, history, ecology, and any others you can find?"

I filled my car with boxes of old books every week for several months. Scott envisioned the house in a Gothic, Addams Family style and furnished it as he and Jed had imagined the house had looked in the twenties.

Three sets of French doors led to the conservatory, the heart of the house. The large windows faced panoramic views of the Berkshire Mountains. The wall of twelve-foot windows, all curved at the top, were the shapes copied by Scott in the design he did for a swimming pool to replace the tennis courts below. Scores of orchids and exotic tropical plants filled the air with a sublime aroma—the smell of France, nature, and expensive fragrance. I came to water them each week.

Overlooking the conservatory was a Juliet balcony in the

ghost room upstairs. Shortly after moving in, Scott heard noises like footsteps and doors closing. Later, many guests also heard strange sounds coming from this room. They agreed the noises must be ghosts. That day, on 9/11 the spirits were my only friends there. I thought of the past, not being able to bear the now or the future.

The charming, intimate dining room had its own fireplace. A fourteen-foot, solid wood nineteenth-century English table was covered with a decorative Egyptian-cotton tablecloth. Two candelabras were placed perfectly for the multiple-course meals Scott and Jed served there, especially on Thanksgiving and Christmas. David and I, Scott and Jed, their friends and neighbors would be arranged equidistant from each other. Candles were used throughout the castle for lighting.

The kitchen had been put through a year's renovation. As much as possible, they kept the integrity of the original style and era with the addition of a hundred-year-old butcher-block table from Paris. There was no plastic anywhere. A second stairway in the kitchen led to two bedrooms upstairs, the kids' room, and the ghost room. Scott loved this house and spent most of his free time working on making it a home. He purchased the authentic European antique furniture from eBay through a local dealer who traveled to countries all over the world. The walls were covered with seventeenth-, eighteenth-, and nineteenth-century paintings, including an 1890s reproduction of Caravaggio's *Love Victorious* from a Hollywood starlet's estate.

I walked around the balcony, past the Steinway baby grand piano Jed had given Scott, to another balcony overlooking the library. I passed through the master bedroom and bath—renovated from three bedrooms and two baths—and across more balconies before entering the ghost room, in the back of the castle. I stared out the window, across the pool and garden to the Berkshire Mountains and beyond. In a daze for several minutes, I attended to a cascading orchid hanging from a small balcony over the conservatory below. I returned down the main stairway, past the library and two more guest rooms.

As I worried about Scott's safety, I watered. Were the twin towers tall enough to hit Scott's loft when they fell? Was he working near there? Lost in the smoke? What if I never saw him alive again? Turning on the TV was an idea too frightening. I finished watering the orchids and left the safe, quiet castle. It was hours later when Scott called me. He and Jed were fine.

Scott and Josiah Howard at the castle in
Palenville, NY, c. 2002, PA

CHAPTER THIRTY-FIVE

JEZEBEL

Scott had given Jed a Bernese Mountain puppy for his birthday. Bernese are a large-sized breed brought by the Romans from the Swiss Alps two-thousand years ago. Jezebel's fur was fluffy, baby-soft, and so smooth and velvety that I wanted to hug the puppy whenever I was near her. Jezebel grew big and fast the first year and spent most of each week at the grand manor house, where Scott took care of her while Jed worked in the city. The puppy cost $3,000, but my son was making $5,000 a day doing makeup in 2008. Two or three days a week were enough to cover his expenses and all the orchids, watches, telescopes, and high-priced designer clothing he collected.

Scott's taste in everything was extreme. Cashmere sweaters as feathery and soft as Jezebel's fur and Egyptian cotton sheets as fine as silk. I kept many of them after he passed, believing he would have wanted me to have his luxuries.

Years later, in the Willow house, sitting on my favorite cozy couch, shoulders covered with the oversized cashmere scarf Scott gave me, I closed my eyes and listened to the birds singing. I imagined my son's scent on a sweater or blanket, the slight fragrance of Moroccan argan oil he used on his hair, a somewhat sweet and musty aroma that when roasted with almonds, tastes a bit like sesame oil.

As I entered memories to revive happy times we had together, I recalled stories from his good friends. In my mind I heard the gentle, tempered voice of my son's best friend, Josiah, describe a day when he remembered Scott Andrew (always using both his names) as "reticent, generous and introspective, who liked *all* clothing—designer, vintage, experimental—every bit of it." One day they were together at an expensive New York City boutique looking around, when Josiah admired a $200 T-shirt. When he returned home, Josiah found six of the T-shirts he'd admired in his backpack, one in each color. Scott had bought them and secretly put them there. He later described Scott as, "selfless, eager to share, and memorable; a cherished, lovely, unforgettable family member."

As I touched the fine wool scarf Scott had chosen for me, I searched for him on Instagram, internet postings, emails from his friends, old letters, and fading memories.

In July, 2001, Scott asked me, "What do you want for your birthday?"

I had quit smoking years before and disapproved of the stench from smoke in the grand manor house in Palenville and the loft in the city. I despised the reek of cigarettes on him and answered, "For you to stop smoking."

"What else?" he replied, immediately after laughing.

"A trip around the world."

Next thing I knew, David and I were booked for Istanbul, Prague, Paris, and beyond; our departure was set for September 13, 2001, two days after the tragic 9/11 attack. Because of all the airport closures, we could not leave the country. We ended up instead in Cape May, New Jersey, a place we'd never been to and was close by. After the airports and borders were reopened, we took a shorter, more limited trip to Prague, Amsterdam, and Paris—skipping Turkey, Greece, and other countries that were suspected of possible terrorist activity.

Scott's generosity was truly astounding. At times he gave as if it cost him nothing. This trip made up for the forgotten birthdays and Mother's Days.

I'm reminded of Scott every day by the expensive gifts he bought for me at Christmas or for no reason, now cherished in our house, closets, garden, and greenhouse. But mostly I delight in simple memories like repotting plants together, sharing the pungent smell of gritty dirt on my fingers.

If I ponder long enough, I can visualize my son coming towards me, dressed in torn blue jeans and a white designer T-shirt, Jezebel by his side, both of them looking happy. Having grieved for so long, it was as if a ray of sunlight was passing through a shadow to warm my skin. I had been trying to pull him out of the heavy darkness inside of me, and here he was, so briefly, like mist over the mountain, quickly thinning before fading away.

Jezebel, along with the three houses and furnishings—the New York City loft, the castle in Palenville, and the LA Dennis Hopper house Jed had bought for Scott on Valentine's Day the year before—all went to Jed in 2013, after he and Scott broke up. They'd been living together for eighteen years.

* * *

Scott stayed sober for twenty years until a back injury resulted in a doctor prescribing OxyContin. The pills opened a door to an escape from pain, a threat every addict knows is always dangerous. He begged Jed and me *not* to send him to another treatment center. I visited Scott each day in the castle, where they were spending weekends while working in New York. Scott went through two weeks of withdrawal, sweating, shaking, squirming—with close-to-death feelings as he fought against the hold that OxyContin had on him. Getting off that drug, he said, had been more difficult than getting off heroin. His second recovery lasted only a few years.

Scott with Jed, Mom and Jezebel at castle,
c. 2006, PA and UNI

CHAPTER THIRTY-SIX

THE BREAKUP

My son rarely confided in me about his relationships with his partner, his father, or his sister, perhaps afraid I would tell others or simply out of a sense of discretion. If he repeated a name several times, I took it to mean he liked that person. If he didn't speak of someone, shrugged, or kept quiet at the mention of them, I assumed he either had no opinion or did *not* like them.

I do know Scott and Jed began an "open" relationship with other partners the last year they were together. One day at the castle, Scott showed me pictures on his phone of a beautiful man. He admitted that he was "in love" and "infatuated" with this bisexual from South America. I cautioned him on both the bisexual part and the risk to his long-term relationship. Scott and Jed had worn rings for years before gay marriage became legal in New York. I knew they were displaying their promise as partners to each other, but after seeing the photos, I sensed trouble and started to notice whether or not they were still wearing the rings. They were not.

In the fall of 2012, we needed to finalize plans for Thanksgiving. The holiday was usually a great event at the castle with Scott and Jed's neighbors, David and me, and any other family members who might be staying with us. Scott called to tell me that Jed wanted to break up and had asked him to leave all three houses. I was shocked and sick, hoping Jed would change his mind. He didn't. Instead, we had Thanksgiving at our house, and Scott invited three friends from the city.

Jed was out of the country and had asked Scott to move out by the end of the year. With so much to dismantle after eighteen years together in three houses, that was not so easy. I was never certain as to why he and Jed broke up but suspected Scott's illness and return to alcohol and drugs the past year was a key issue. It started with a simple glass of wine at the previous Christmas table at the castle. I commented on it, but Scott just smiled.

"It's Christmas," he said. Christmas was always Scott's favorite holiday. I was sad but ignored it and later asked Jed to keep his wine cellar locked.

From there, Scott's downfall was slow but steady. I was tired of pointing out the times he lifted a glass of alcohol. His work and health unraveled as he was often too ill to take on a makeup job. His doctor gave him drugs for his liver disease while I wondered if he knew about the drinking. I stopped commenting on his drinking but never stopped noticing. Scott spent Christmas with us. He seemed happy to be out of the relationship but must have been worried where he would go.

On New Year's Eve, Scott had a party at the Crosby loft in New York while Jed was in Europe. Scott then spent weeks in bed at the castle with depression before packing up some clothes and personal items. But by March 2013, he had nowhere to go. Jed called me several times.

"Why can't you get your son to move out?" he yelled at me in January.

"After eighteen years, I think this is *YOUR* problem." I answered angrily.

Jed had purchased the Dennis Hopper Hollywood Hills house as a gift for Scott the previous Valentine's Day. I thought surely it would go to Scott. It didn't.

I gave him business cards from three lawyers who could possibly advise him, but Scott was unable to help himself. Gay marriage had been legal since 2011—yet for some reason, they chose to not marry. After years living in luxury, my son was homeless. He stayed at our house in February while David and I were in Florida, then found an apartment in Long Island City. Due to his inability to work because of a Hep C flare up and medical bills, Scott was almost broke by then. Jed paid the six month's rent required for the apartment lease. The next year, Scott's health got worse as his drinking continued.

Scott in NYC, c. 2010, UNI

Scott, c. 2000 – '08, PA and UNI

CHAPTER THIRTY-SEVEN

A FEELING

I had scheduled a busy week ahead, starting Monday, June 9, 2014. First was a consultation with my meditation teacher.

Odd, I thought, why am I unable to relax? Perhaps I was worrying about my doctor's appointment afterwards. It was a routine checkup, but I wanted to address the stress-level I had been experiencing, which I attributed to recent problems and resignations on the board of directors that I chaired at the Woodstock Artists Association.

While waiting in my doctor's office, I spoke with Andrea, my son's friend and gardener when he lived at the castle.

"We have the same doctor, I see. How's Scott been?" she asked.

Turning to face her I answered with a tremble in my voice, "I don't know. He hasn't called lately or answered my emails or phone messages. He has a doctor's appointment today at Mt. Sinai in the city. I'm worried about him."

A deep, nauseating apprehension arose throughout my body and when my doctor called me in, I wondered, "Why *hasn't* he called?" He often waited days before returning my call, but it had been longer this time.

Going through the next few days somewhat dazed, my fears and suspicions continued. Tuesday and Wednesday were filled with a dancercise class, writing group, shopping, art submissions, and important meetings at the museum to discuss contracts, resignations, planning for the library fair, and the annual senior lunch at the community center.

I had never been busier. By Thursday, an unusual sense of growing trepidation was building in me, verging on panic. When I went to a memorial for a friend, scheduled from 2:00–6:00, I couldn't get out of there soon enough. "Strange," I thought. It was a lovely day and memorial services never bothered me before. Why was I experiencing this insufferable dread and foreboding? Again, I tried calling and emailing Scott.

"Doesn't he often go several days before returning calls?" David asked.

"Yes, but …" I was still distraught.

My calendar showed a talk and fundraising dinner Friday night at White Pines, the historical home of another arts organization I had been invited to attend. I asked my husband to pick me up at 9:00 p.m. but sensed before then what felt like excruciating boredom or some unnatural anxiety. I went outside to get cell service, hoping to have him pick me up sooner. I glanced at the multitude of stars above and thought of Scott, how he loved looking through his many telescopes on a clear night.

"Something must be wrong with Scott," I thought, afraid to say it out loud. When we returned home, I checked the answering machine. It showed eighteen calls. Most were from Jed or Luke, Scott's ex-partner and friend saying, "Call me." My heart raced. Was Scott in jail again? I called Patricia, Scott's work friend, who was one of the last messages.

She asked me to sit down, then reported, "I'm so sorry to be the one to tell you, Pat. Scott is dead."

My legs buckled. I screamed, *"NOOOOO,"* My breath gave out as I stumbled to the chair. A terrifying and unbearably sick feeling came to me as my husband ran to help. He turned on the speaker phone for more details as I alternated between screaming and crying.

"No one could get hold of him since Sunday," Patricia continued. "John, Scott's friend and neighbor, asked the police to break into his apartment."

The coroner ruled that Scott had died from hemorrhaging blood on Monday, June 9th, five days before he was found, the day he didn't show up to see his doctor, the day I had started going through the motions of my life.

My son was found in a pool of blood, on a cold floor, alone. The blood and his death were from his bleeding out and I believed exacerbated by the trial drug Sovaldi Scott had been taking to treat his Hepatitis C. Not yet on the market, the drug had cost him $1,000 a pill, daily for three months.

After his death, it was discovered from the last blood test he'd had three days before he died that he was indeed cured of Hep C. His doctor said, "It wasn't the drug that killed him." I was shocked that he said this, since early trials had shown a percentage of the first one-hundred Sovaldi volunteers had died from bleeding out.

The police allowed us into his apartment a few days after he was found. I had to prove I was his mother before David and I were finally given his keys. We cleaned up the blood, packed some of his personal items, cell phone, and a large bag of drugs, all prescribed by doctors, and left the Long Island City apartment with its balcony view of Manhattan, the city he loved and lived in for more than half his life of fifty years.

While David sorted through legalities and paperwork, we both dealt with bank visits, accountants, lawyers, calls to credit card companies and services on the internet. Uber, Spotify, PayPal, and other accounts had to be cancelled. We found a funeral director to arrange the cremation.

I also needed to find places for the furniture, clothes, makeup, watches, and household items. We gave Scott's bed and some of his clothing to Luke, Scott's close friend and business partner. We had several weeks to clean and empty the apartment. With Jed's help, we made arrangements for the New York memorial, and I bought a gravesite in Woodstock for his remains. I wanted to keep Scott close to me.

Scott with David Ekroth, c. 2010, PA

PART III.

Afterlife:

* * *

The Japanese Stone Orchid, *Dendrobium moniliforme*.
Large Royalty used it to perfume clothing.
Blooms in early spring, fragrant flowers are usually white.

Author at gravesite, Woodstock, NY, c. 2016,
photo by David Ekroth

CHAPTER THIRTY-EIGHT

SAYING GOODBYE

The day was warm and sunny, a rarity from the usual cold, wet spring in Woodstock. I drove up beyond the top of the hill and parked in a shady spot. No one was in the cemetery. No one, it seems, is ever there. I walked over to my destination with violets, notebook, and blanket, carefully watching to not disturb those resting underground. There was a scent of grass and wildflowers mixed with a fleeting sweet fragrance from a neighbor's flowering tree. Finding my destination, I placed the violets in a depression in front of the stone. I laid out the blanket, removed my shoes, and opened my notebook.

"Are you at peace?" I asked.

"Can you hear the birds singing or feel the warm sun?"

Other than the birds, there was only silence. A lone, haunting chirp continued nonstop among happy tweets and small peeps from others. The air was filled with so much life that I could not fathom silence underneath the ground. Believing that I was just unable to hear his voice, I laid my head on the stone and imagined Scott telling me he was happy to be in nature, so close to home.

"Don't be sad," I sensed his voice whisper, "I'm in good company."

Originally founded to separate the rich from the poor, the Woodstock Artists Cemetery was my choice for Scott. I wanted him near me and our friends, both alive and dead, in the company of his equals. This small cemetery is located a block north of the

Village Green in Woodstock, New York, on an unkempt sloping hill with patchy grass mixed with chicory and wild strawberry, and encircled by woods. The ashes of my son are two feet below the surface under a gravestone that replaced a sparkling grey granite marker gifted by our local stone yard.

"No charge, it's our pleasure," they told my husband when he asked for a temporary stone. With a black marker, we wrote "Scott" on it one lovely fall day, a few years after Scott's death. The name disappeared over the winter, a reminder that I would soon have to make up my mind on what to properly inscribe on a permanent gravestone, one that would outlast me and most of our friends. Makeup Artist? Beloved Son and Friend? Or simply Scott Andrew Mortenson, 1963–2014?

The site I chose is next to Lilo Raymond, a photographer of light and beauty. Certainly, she and Scott have made a connection. I thought of her photographs of sunlit curtains on shadowed windows, a perfect backdrop for the women whose faces were exquisitely made up by Scott. Among other famous artists nearby are Milton Avery, Phillip Guston, and the founders of Byrdcliffe, our local artist colony. My poet friend and onetime housemate Janine Pommy Vega is in a nearby grave and had once written: "I dreamt of a place, a home town where you planted your feet in the earth instead of waving them in the air in surrender."

Hundreds of other creative souls are buried close by. It pleased me that the earlier intentions to separate the wealthier summer residents from commoners had been replaced by a mix of poets and artists. Scott fit in with everyone and, most certainly, would be popular among the spirits.

I strolled carefully back to my car after an undisturbed half hour reading names on the gravestones. Hearing a birdcall, I turned to see a bright red cardinal flying over Scott's grave. He swooped up and down as if in deference, acknowledging our visit. I put my shoes back on and sat on the slope next to the car as I looked over the earlier rich residents and the top-of-the-hill artists.

I Hoped they were all communicating with my son and enjoying his company.

*　*　*

The next day after breakfast, I was neatly stacking wood as yellow leaves clung to giant cold trees, when Scott's image floated over the wood pile. He came to tell me he had felt my hand on his gravestone the day before at the Artists Cemetery. Tall grasses swayed next to me, bending towards the sun behind him. I felt the wood in my moldy-gloved hands become weightless.

The pleasure I felt was familiar; the same as when he first appeared after having passed years earlier, when I was looking at the framed collages on the wall in my bedroom or when I heard his voice. "Why not do more of this work?"

For a year in my dreams and visions, he'd continued to unforgivingly pressure me to give up writing about him and do my art. But I had been stuck in grief. Transfixed, I dropped the wood, took off the gloves and stepped closer, hoping for some integration, wanting to join him or have him join me back in life in full color—solid, alive, strong, healthy, and as loving as my memories of him remained.

I remembered a scene from David's and my shared birthday party one summer. I had laid out some books on a coffee table that would interest Scott, *Russian Constructivism*, *The Illustrated World of Thoreau*, *The Paris I Love*. They were displayed to entice his interest. He picked up the Paris book, slouched against a pillow and cushioned his left foot on the massive round coffee table. His right foot hung over his knee as he read while guests mingled at the party. It was as if he was waiting to transport himself while lingering right there, at that moment, in that book, learning and adding to his world of knowledge.

As we scurried around, introducing friends to family, family to neighbors, and chatted about insignificant happenings or facts that mattered little—Scott stayed deep in the past with long dead artists and writers from decades ago. Even after being interrupted to meet or welcome whomever I brought to him, he would hold onto what he was reading while conversing with the guest as if to keep in his mind the discovery from what he had just read.

The memory faded, along with his image. I moved away from the wood pile and went into my studio.

Scott in Woodstock, Minneapolis and friend
at pool, c. 1997 – 2005, PA

CHAPTER THIRTY-NINE

LIFE MASK

Holding the heavy concrete plaster life mask in my hands, I looked into the angelic vision of what was once my son's silent, serene face. The solidly cast molded mask was made several years before Hepatitis C or the drugs Scott took for the disease changed his handsomely chiseled face. We found the mask on the window ledge in his Long Island City apartment a week after his death, when my husband and I had only twenty minutes, with a police escort, to retrieve important papers proving we were next of kin. In New York City, a death is held "suspicious" until the autopsy report. I immediately grabbed a shoe box, and with crumpled paper as padding, carefully and quickly placed the sleeping face in its coffin as my tears flowed, knowing the mask would become a treasured object.

I gave the expensive watches and jewelry to a jeweler friend who sold most of them through his store in New York. Scott's clothes went to his friends, to exclusive resale shops on the upper East Side, and to another friend's daughter who sold used designer items on the web. I kept some of the clothes and makeup for myself and gave the new makeup to Kim, nieces, friends, their daughters, and a few sons who were in process or had already transgendered.

The Steinway baby grand piano Jed had given to Scott was sold to a musician, and the telescopes and astronomy equipment went to professional astronomers. The new observatory Scott had purchased from Australia, still wrapped in packaging, was meant to be installed by the pool behind the castle. It was gifted to a college in upstate New York. The centuries-old paintings he had collected were given to auction houses, destined for art collectors who admire Renaissance paintings. All these precious treasures were relatively easy to part with. The life mask however, will always be with me, feeding my soul as it portrays the core of his spirit, now settled solidly in my heart.

I lost part of my "self" following Scott's death. As if my reason for *being* died along with him. He was so much of who I was, and I believed I'd become some of the best parts of him. My self-assurance was his. My creativity, taught *to* him, came back *through* him in so many ways. I searched for the "new" in my studio and began a quest to incorporate his ideas and unconventional lifestyle into my work. I used his artwork and images of him in my collages.

Since I was so young when he was born, Scott and I really grew up together. While he was in his crib, I played classical music over and over. After his nap he and I experimented with the Holiday Magic Makeup—a pyramid scheme his father had invested in to make extra money. We didn't know at that time how famous Scott would become as a makeup artist, although there were several clues.

While he was a toddler Scott had started putting on makeup after watching me. When I was sewing, we both played with the buttons, zippers, spools of thread, and piles of fabric. It was in the late sixties and early seventies that he started dressing up in my or my mother's clothes, putting on plays, or posing for photos. We gave Scott the 8mm movie camera and his first telescope. When he was ten, I started taking art, photography, and video classes at the local college. Scott saw me photograph and videotape women around the subject of sex and gender identity. He asked to go with me to the graveyard, and while I photographed my friend Lorna, dressed in vintage clothes and draped dramatically over a concrete stone tomb, Scott observed, moving around both of us while he filmed.

Eventually, a few years after his death, I began to have a desire to create again. One day while in the studio, I opened the shoe box and circled around it, as he'd done with Lorna and me at the cemetery, searching for just the right light. I cautiously lifted the mask out of its coffin and added a colorful see-through scarf around harsh jagged edges, to soften it. Dancing with my son, I began to find my "self" again, feeling his gentle closeness, hearing his piano music, smelling the hint of the Santa Maria Herb Water from Italy that he wore. Scott was becoming my muse again, as I was once his. I grabbed my camera.

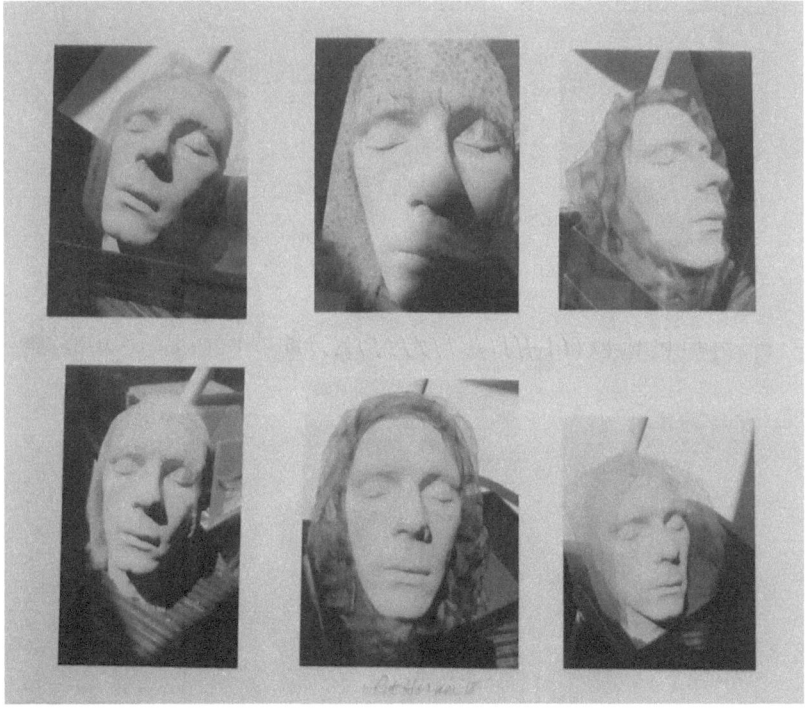

Collage, *Lifemask*, 2018, by Pat Horner

Magazine pages of Scott's makeup, c. 1996 – 2012, UNI

Scott working, c. 2000, UNI

CHAPTER FORTY

THE MAKEUP CASE

Scott's last makeup case wasn't opened for more than a year after his death. It was a hard-shelled, silver case with the red, square design of a large X over the word *Titan*. Shaped like a replica of an Air Stream trailer, it had the quality and look of an unbreakable exterior with a flawless frame, not unlike my son.

It was time for me to face his life. I opened the case to find a dozen smaller see-through cases and several leather, velvet, and flannel bags. Opening the first one felt like an intrusion into a secret: Scott's trade as a makeup artist. He was in here. I was certain. Locked away in this case, when I needed them most, were many options. Not the cosmetics but his art, his tools, him. The Cinema Secrets foundation, black lipstick, eyeliner pencils, false eyelashes, lip tar, makeup palettes, sparkle lip glosses and powder, eye glitter and shimmering gels, cream crayons, and dozens of best quality brushes. All of these would be embraced, given away, or used in my own art.

The first red lipstick labeled Chanel was half-used and the shade of Liza Minnelli's lips in the Mac Cosmetics advertisement he worked on. It was also the same color as the blood I found on his bathroom and kitchen floors after he had passed. The next tube, a neutral shade, was the color of our skin, his and mine. It was possible that one of these bags was filled with favorite cosmetics for an individual client he particularly admired, one of the models or actresses he considered a friend. I held a gold stardust powder container, knowing he had used it on many models. It was all in there. His love and his art.

I looked for clues in each of the cases that stored the powders, so smooth and delicate—the brushes, so flexible and soft. I brushed my face with several, remembering the day he did my makeup at Alcone, the store for professionals that he managed in Manhattan before becoming so successful. I saw his long, thin fingers and the skull ring he wore on his right hand sparkling with different colored diamonds. His eyes searched for every flaw or imperfection on my face.

I remembered the steadiness of his hand, two years before he became ill, before the prescription drugs made his hands shake, as he applied eyeliner and mascara with a detailed line of the brush on my eyes and lips. Magically, he turned me into a beautiful exotic creature.

There was another red, this one I believed was the color of his liver—and the next-darker red, I imagined, the Hepatitis C virus in his body. Both reminded me of the wine I pleaded with him not to drink. There were also bright pinks, the shade of what I knew was his sweet, good heart.

I continue to put on red lipstick and a touch of eyeliner on days when I go out, always wanting a bit of him with me.

CHAPTER FORTY-ONE

ORCHIDS

At times during his life with Jed, Scott had more than two-hundred orchids. When living in Woodstock he made a greenhouse in the basement of the rented Willow house, five minutes up the mountain from me. He put in high-powered lights and rolls of plastic to keep the humidity in. It felt like a tropical garden. Both the castle in Palenville and the Soho apartment in New York had indoor solariums and, upon moving into the castle, Scott turned the garage under the guest house into an arboretum for cattleyas, cymbidiums, epiphytes, terrestrials, hybrids, and exotic air orchids. During weeks when Scott was working, I drove the four miles up the road—then later, twenty miles to the castle—to water the orchids. One winter, when Scott and Jed were in the city, the electricity went out for several days. Without heat and light, most of the two-hundred orchids died. He had given me several dozen babies from his orchids over the years, and I was happy to give some back to him. We spent days together, repotting.

The summer after he died, I looked out my dining room window at four *Encyclia cochleatas* (clamshell orchids) that Scott and I had divided a few months before he passed away. All in bloom, they had dark purple, nearly black, shell-like lips with a white spot toward the center and lime-green tepals falling away from the base like ribbons. These plants got on well with the bright fuchsia cattleyas Scott had given me fifteen years before, which were finished blooming now. Several others had buds on them and I awaited their flowering.

Most of the orchids I have left flower every year. Even the orchid Jed sent to Scott's memorial bloomed again for years.

* * *

One spring in the early twenties, some dying daffodils peeked over my computer in front of me. The forsythia picked from my own bushes and magnolia snapped from a neighbor's tree were also wilting in the living room. Thousands of people were losing their lives each week from the Coronavirus pandemic, and while it rained, I cried. The empty space between things became more relevant than the space filled every day with so much death. I searched for connections.

I thought of lighter days ahead—bringing spring flowers and my orchids outside for the summer and fall, repotting the *Cattleya* and spider orchids Scott had given me one day in summer after he led me up to the wooded land behind the castle.

"We'll get lost," I said, knowing he had recently moved in and wouldn't have had a chance to become familiar with the expanse of the forest. Laughing, he kept ahead with excitement, searching the ground as if following a trail to the possibility of wonder. Earlier, he had described to me the wild orchids he had seen there and wanted to show me. Scott pointed to one. I reached for it as though it were simply a wild flower.

"*NO!*" he yelled with a *"rape the earth"* look on his face as I went to pick it. Shocked at my ignorance, he kneeled, as if in prayer, reaching with delicate fingers to reveal the fragile beauty of the blossoms from under the greens covering them. While protecting this tiny gem, he relayed the story of a Minnesota rescue team he had read about where wild orchids found in a ditch would soon be excavated for a new road. "Orchid lovers from the state and beyond came to dig them up and moved them into the woods nearby." He explained.

"You can get off alcohol, drugs ... food and cars, but once you're hooked on orchids, you're finished. You never get off orchids ... never." Joe Krenisch, an orchid grower from New York wrote.

Years later, in our house in Willow, the last of the spider blossoms on the orchid Scott gave me withered and drooped as the scale insects weakened it to their own ends. I turned the plant to find evidence of possible snaillike homes of the sneaky pests that I may have missed the week before, when I noticed sticky residue—a sign of their prolific reproduction. As the blossom fell to a final death, I searched for the brown cave-like incrustations that the scale affix to the plant in order for their young to suck the juices from the blossoms. They multiply faster than my weekly watering and checking can keep up with.

The light green petals contorted and scrolled to their tips, only an inch-and-a-half long. I soaked a paper towel with soapy water and picked off hopefully the last of the scale's brown shells. The drips of sticky syrup reminded me of the sweetness of my son. A dead brown flower caught in one of the leaves hung on for a graceful end—its proof of existence, of being. The lone bud at the tip of the fifteen-inch stem looked brown and would likely die, but I left it there, as I have let so many of Scott's things stay in the house, somehow hoping that the life of each of them will keep part of him or my memory of him alive.

Scott with me and Jed, c. 1998 – 2006, PA,
David Ekroth and UNI

CHAPTER FORTY-TWO

SCOTT'S THINGS AND RING

Immediately after sorting his clothes and personal items from his apartment, I started wearing and using Scott's sweaters and cosmetics. If I couldn't have him with me, I could keep what he wore, the makeup he used on his clients, the oil he used in his hair; their fragrance brought him back, if only momentarily. His cashmere sweaters kept me warm but also kept me close to what few molecules were left from his being alive. I couldn't part with the many hairbrushes he had had, as, each time I used one, I was and still am reminded of his long, thin, lovely head of hair flowing from a high forehead, surrounding his beautiful face.

I put on the ring that he wore on his left hand while making the YouTube beauty lesson videos. The ring has a skull on it with diamonds covering the forehead and more diamonds as eyes and under the chin. A few of the stones are shaded differently from the others, a light violet in the eyes and a soft gentle green under the chin. In daylight, the sparkling stones inject energetic, laser-like messages to my memories. The gold band, marked with an abstract design that seems a language I cannot decipher, holds the ring perfectly on my finger. It fits several different fingers on each of my hands, which I take as a sign that Scott wanted me to have it. I somehow sensed he needed to connect with me.

The ring was found in the back of a bedside drawer after he passed away, I knew it was a significant present left for me. My son's quintessence was in this skull, shining as *he* had shined in life. Scott's friend, Luke, when seeing the ring on my hand, asked, "Where did you find this? We spent hours searching for it,"

I explained the story of finding the ring and Luke said that he and Scott had thought it was stolen. The ring meant a lot to Scott. Jed had given it to him as a token of their relationship long before they split up.

It was a traumatic breakup—with anger and accusations. Whether it was Scott being ill, drinking too much, or both of them having other lovers, the relationship came to a devastatingly hurtful end for Scott. Jed had shut him out of his homes—the homes Scott had made for them both by furnishing, decorating and caring for each with expertise and love. Scott received little compensation and months later was finally dropped from the business. Jed stopped representing Scott the year before he died.

* * *

I wore the ring for a few years until the skull turned black in a Florida hot tub one winter. I decided that it had been enough. I couldn't bring Scott back or erase the heartbreak of his painful split. Jed had gone on to another relationship and married his young lover, then divorced him for another young model.

Jed still lives in the castle on the hill and, perhaps, I hope, is visited by Scott's ghost. I had little contact with him other than when David and I removed Scott's belongings in twenty boxes, along with his astronomy equipment, telescopes and conservatory.

Six years after Scott passed, I received a package of photographs from Jed.

"I hope you guys are staying safe and healthy! While cleaning up the house, I came across this pack of photos. I'm sure that you'd like to have them. All the best! Sincerely, Jed."

I was surprised and pleased that he sent them. Most were of Scott in drag, some were duplicates I had but there were also new ones. I wrote a thank-you note and wished him well.

Scott in Paris, c. 1991, PA

Scott with family, Ft. Pierce, Florida, 2014.

CHAPTER FORTY-THREE

LEGACY

David and I were wintering in Florida when Scott came to visit. We didn't know it was to be during the final months before Scott passed. He brought his friend Luke, and they played tennis with my nieces, sister, brother-in-law, David, and me. It was the first time Scott played a series of matches and, though he wasn't great at hitting the ball, he tried for hours to return balls—laughing and teasing me and Luke, neither of us tennis players. I noticed he had gained weight.

After returning to New York, I dreamt Scott had taken up tennis seriously. He bought a Yamaha racket, rented a court in Long Island City, and practiced. On his way home in a rental car, he put in a CD of classics and sang along with the Byrds about wanting to be a rock star. Dressed in a torn white T-shirt and army-green shorts cut off to the knee, he had a tattoo of three piano keys on his upper arm. He was once again thin and beautiful. Scott was wearing the scull ring and moving his fingers to a beat that he heard from the tennis ball going back and forth on the court. He remembered past drag shows he had starred in. I seemed to be dreaming *his* dream of performing.

I imagined Scott thought playing tennis would get him in shape. In *his* dream, he envisioned a piano onstage, a trumpet player, and three tennis players assisting. The Rock & Roll music of the sixties would be background for him. He was in drag, with big, light-blond hair and makeup applied, with drawn eyes and red lips.

Partially awake, I remembered Scott dressed in a pink paisley-design pant suit, prepping his spiked blond wig, and jewelry—large black circle earrings dotted with rhinestones—posing as if he wasn't being watched, turning first left, then right, carefully, so as not to look at the audience. Back in my dream, Scott made a few arm gestures, demure faces, and provocative poses as he slipped elegantly in front of the piano. On the arm of each tennis player was a tattoo of shiny black-lacquer trumpets that matched the Steinway baby grand. The players transformed their tennis rackets to trumpets half way through the show when the rock music changed to jazz. He was having fun, now backed by grown-up friends instead of the family and neighborhood kids he remembered from his youth. Scott's wig came off and he became himself. My dream ended with his performing Debussy's *Clair de Lune* on the piano.

After awakening, I longed for him to finish his life as the goddess he had been on stage. I needed him to finalize the life he dreamt of, dressing up one last time, performing his music, projecting his gorgeous self, loving everyone, uplifting us all with an example from his life.

I suspected before he died that Scott wanted to do drag again. He had stopped when he moved in with his boyfriend twenty years earlier. I believed that drag was Scott's way to fully present his inner being by expressing himself as an artist, performer, musician—not simply as a he or she but all in one.

* * *

Halfway through working on this book, Scott appeared to me in another vision. I was sitting upstairs in the sun-dappled room when he appeared. He was dressed in the tuxedo he had worn to the yearly New York City auction for the Center of Photography at Woodstock. Jed had recently become a board member and invited David and me. Scott wore his hair down and had grown a short moustache.

In the vision, I asked my son what his legacy should be. Scott looked down, paused a minute, raised his head, and closed his eyes.

"I want other gays and those questioning their identities to know that being different is a gift—a special flower, jewel, or star yet to be discovered—a unique thing of beauty and love." Scott opened his vibrant, moist eyes and stared deeply into my face as he continued.

"You tried to teach me this but I still felt you wanted me to change. I thought you wanted me to be *healed* when you sent me to the gay therapist at seventeen, before I even came out. Then you made me go back to Minneapolis to live with my father, who you knew was embarrassed by me—by my failures, my differentness, my inability to continue in school or get good grades or dress like the other kids at Washburn High—of my not having a real girlfriend, only friends who were girls—of my staying out late at night to look at the stars or hear a band I liked—of my skipping school, skipping out of the house, skipping the suburban way of life."

But of course, these are *my* words and *my* guilt coming from a place of shame. In deep corners of my DNA there is the Irish and Swedish inadequate self-esteem gene. It comes from being a too poor, too different, new kid on the block—town or country—with deep feelings rooted in me, setting up my beliefs long before Scott was born.

My mother's family came from Sweden and settled in Madison, a small town in Minnesota. Her father was a contractor who built the court house, opera house, and other prominent buildings. Her mother died of consumption when she was thirteen. After her four older sisters all married "well," my mother married an Irish, nonpracticing Roman Catholic alcoholic from a large family who had emigrated from Ireland and moved to Graceville, a small town near Madison.

She married at twenty-seven, an age considered "old maid" at that time. Shame. They were poor and lived with their four children in a two-room apartment, sharing a bathroom with six other renters. My father was well-known at the bar and when I, the youngest child, was sent in to get him, humiliating disgrace crept in as it did when I saw him beat up my mother.

Even when we moved to a nicer place in a better neighborhood, the shame followed. Whenever friends came over, I would not want them in the bedroom I shared with my three siblings. They would have to come to the front door and pass by my father, sitting in his underwear in the living room. I started dating at fifteen. When I had to introduce a boyfriend to him in order to go out, it was extremely embarrassing. I was mortified.

My father died when I was sixteen. My mother had to drop out of nurses training to work in a *laundry* because it paid more than nursing. This brought on further dishonor. Then I got pregnant and ran away to Arizona with Scott's father. We returned to my mother's house just months before Kennedy's assassination. Even *that* piled on more Irish shame.

My mother's behavior was far from helpful. It was deeply embarrassing when she yelled at a black friend who visited from school, "Don't you ever step on this porch again or come to this neighborhood!" Deep humiliation.

I tried to overcome the prejudice my family and teachers attempted to instill in me. When I made friends with the few Native Americans or Blacks in our neighborhood as a way to balance the inequality I observed around me, I suffered from my parents' disapproval. By college I was finally able to have open relationships with other races while raising my children to be accepting.

Scott always avoided prejudices, stereotypes or intolerances. He seemed to love everyone.

My vision that day ended with Scott's sound advice. "I want you to write that it's okay for young teenagers to follow their path; to embrace their feelings; to experiment with their interests creatively, sexually, and emotionally. Parents should trust their children, as they do their brothers, sisters, cousins, and friends—and accept them as unique and *equal* individuals, helping them find a path of their own, a life of their own."

Scott, c. 2008, UNI

Scott with Jed, me and cousin Sandy, c. 1994 - 2006, PA and UNI

CHAPTER FORTY-FOUR

LAST MEAL

I walked into the restaurant my friend had suggested with a sense of apprehension. Of what I did not know, yet it felt like fear. Lured to a table closest to the door and by the window with glaring light, I hoped that my friend from an earlier writing workshop would agree to sit at this location. I arrived several minutes early, sat down and watched the few people walking by outside the window. A creek was nearby, but I couldn't hear it. Sunlight streamed through windows, creating shadows on the table. I opened my notebook and wrote the scene as if it might mean something later, as if writing it would dissipate my sense of unease.

My friend entered, saw me, and pointed to another table, also by a window, facing the street. He asked, "Is *that one* okay?" I calculated it would be just a few steps further to the exit and agreed, as I moved there.

He slipped the manuscript towards me saying, "I read it five times and I couldn't help but copyedit the whole thing."

"Seventy-five pages? Five times? Copyedited?" I exclaimed. I hoped to hear praise from him as I had the first time he'd read it, six months earlier.

"I did eight pages of notes and we can go over them or not. Do you want to order?" He called the waiter over, and we ordered soup.

"You're uncannily able to uncover the poignant aspects of your son's life," my friend said as we ate, mostly in silence while

I scanned his notes. I knew his time was limited and that he was on a lunch break.

My stomach felt queasy, and I hoped eating would calm my apprehension. I heard loud chatter from the table in the middle of the restaurant. Looking over, I saw a younger man with two older people, maybe parents. In a flash, I remembered. *Oh*, that was the exact table Scott was sitting at with me and my husband, the final hours we were together. It was the last time we shared a meal before he took the bus back to the city. It was Mother's Day 2014, only a few weeks before he died. The restaurant, Joshua's, was busy that day. We had to wait to be seated, wait to order, wait for our food.

Scott had looked tired, his face swollen. I wondered if it was from the drugs he had taken for Hep C or from alcohol. He ordered several glasses of wine, which came right away. Noticing my displeasure at this, he made the excuse, "They're small glasses."

We ate our food in silence. Earlier that morning, Scott and I had done our usual plant shopping, a ritual we enjoyed since he'd moved up to his weekend house in Woodstock years before. Every Mother's Day he would help pick out and buy plants for my garden and decks. He took several hours choosing the perfect varieties as he named each by both botanical and common attributions.

And here I was, five years later, in the same restaurant, having unconsciously avoided it all that time. The fear finally faded from my middle, and another layer of grief vanished from my memories. I shared the revelation of that last day with Scott, along with my longtime avoidance of Joshua's restaurant with my friend.

"Write it!" he said forcefully, a directive, an order to write the story.

"I don't know if I can," I replied.

"Write it," he said again as he got up to leave. "We've got a plan?" he asked, referring to the "Last Meal with Scott" story.

"Yes," I promised.

There is a biology to aging, one which explains incorporating plans for lost memory, for slower responses, for simply wanting or needing more rest. A younger person could have written this book in a year. Now, in my seventies, it has taken five years and will assuredly take longer.

As I left Joshua's, I remembered the day I'd kissed and said goodbye to my son for the last time, a few steps away at the bus stop. The last time his mouth went to mine, the last time our eyes were on each other. Fifty years at an end, which I couldn't know that day.

"I won't see you for a while. I love you," were his last words to me.

"I love you, take care of yourself, please," were my last words to him. He waved from the window while David and I waved back.

Our longest, closest relationship, a love so unconditional that the idea, even now, of it being over shocks me. I may learn to accept his death yet will never believe he is gone. As with my garden at the end of winter, I remain vulnerable, waiting for nature to take its course.

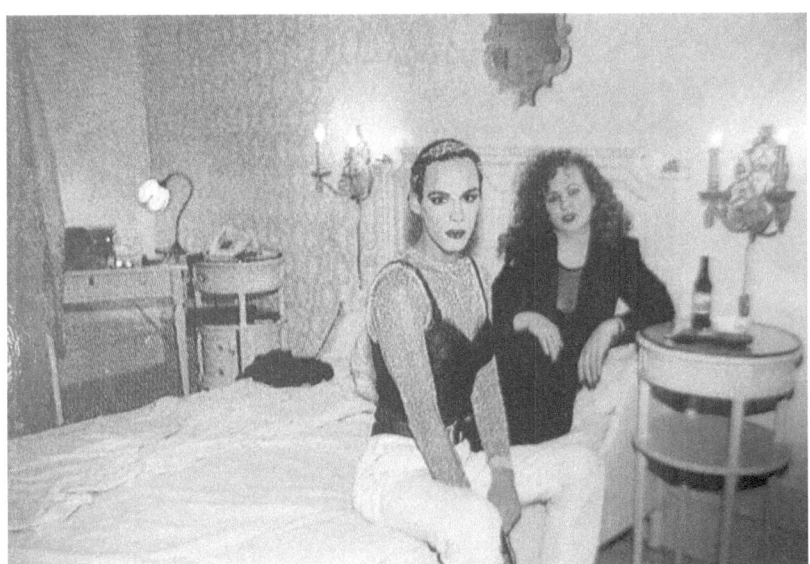

Misty and Nan in Berlin hotel, 1992, Photo by Joey Gabriel

Misty with two cigarettes, NYC, c. 1991, Photo by Linda Simpson

CHAPTER FORTY-FIVE

LETTING GO

I was numb for months after Scott passed but eventually returned to a "normal" place, though it is hard to believe I will ever be the same again. Immobility was necessary the first year. It was a protective cloak to the reality of having lost my only son, my firstborn, my best friend. The second year, denial set in, and if I didn't look at his pictures or life mask, I wouldn't feel the pain. If I didn't write about him, did it really happen? I tried to move on but found myself isolating, staying away from friends and gatherings.

David and I had married in 2010, and without him, my grief would have frozen inside me. He fed me when I couldn't make meals. He got me out of the house when I only wanted to stay close to Scott's belongings, photographs, and comforting cashmere throws. David took care of all my and Scott's paperwork, insurance, and taxes. This freed me to discover how I could heal.

I had to forgive myself for not being able to intervene more in Scott's diseases. I felt anguish and sorrow for the loss of him.

My son's first memorial was held in a studio in Chelsea where he'd often worked on photo shoots. Seventy-five of his colleagues and friends attended including several young talented creatives Scott had mentored. I knew he mattered to so many and was deeply optimistic that others wanted to hear Scott's story. I announced then that I would write a book about his life. I felt a duty to help others who would never be able to meet him.

Scott's second memorial was held in Minneapolis where

another 75 friends and family came. I was often comforted later while reading the notes from those who attended and wrote in the guest books their feelings about Scott:

"His contagious warmth and spirit, so clearly loved, enthusiastic, inspiring, generous heart, kind, creative free soul, among the fabulous, already an angel, friendly and graceful, calm and peaceful, sweetness in his eyes, always so accepting, beautiful energy, source of warmth and light, comfortable shoulder, sweet hug, pushing us towards excellence and excitement, leaving a gentle whisper in the air, amazing, real, good, irreplaceable, gem, golden spirit, love, laughter, compassion, serene beauty, humble, grounded, calm, kind, sincere, unique magic."

Acknowledgment of losing Scott began to creep in when my studio called to me. It felt natural to add Scott to my artwork. I collaged his photos onto my paintings. I photographed my son's concrete mask. Scott's likeness, so perfectly formed from his handsome face, was substantial enough to last my lifetime and more. Quickly working with the stone face added conflict and chaos to my routine. I felt guilt for using Scott in my art yet feared returning to a phase of denial. I wondered if I could handle the idea of the mask or photographs being all I had left of him. Could I share these with others in my art?

Conscious of the possibility that the world would forget Scott urged me on as I continued to promise myself and others to put his life into a book and into my art—to keep him alive. Photographing his face in stone freed me to look deeper into the place where he resides now—in all beauty and in the orchids he so loved.

I see him everywhere. He is in the veil I use in my studio and the veil that I look through to the outside. He is inside of me, everywhere I go. And from the notes, letters, calls, and emails I received, I know he will remain in the hearts of others who knew him. We are better people because of him, more loving, more accepting, more generous to each other and all those we meet.

There was so much I still didn't know about Scott. Initially, I searched for more of him on Facebook and other internet postings, emails from his friends after he passed, old letters I wrote to him that he saved, the few letters he wrote to me, my journal entries from years ago—although it was painful to read accounts of my anger and his bad behavior. I didn't want to explore his dark side or any unpleasant thoughts, only good ones dusted off from inside my memories, from times we shared. Fifty years of memories emerged in no significant order—a collage of images, poses, smiles, and moments I treasure from our lives together.

Recognizing denial and bargaining in my thoughts, I sent the dark pain flowing up and out to where I imagined Scott lives—in the air, trees, mountains, water, and sky. I took his lessons and the example of living his life and his creativity forward, honoring the grief I leave behind.

Misty Doing Her Makeup. Paris 1991, Photo by Nan Goldin

Misty and Joey at Hornstrasse, Berlin, 1992, Photo by Nan Goldin

CHAPTER FORTY-SIX

ACCEPTANCE

There is a meditation room upstairs in the Willow house with a cathedral ceiling and triangular windows that flood with light from the sun's rays. I sat on a cushioned chair in the bay window, watching the water rush by in our backyard stream swollen from a recent rain. While meditating on bringing Scott back in order to let him go, I sensed a cloud pass over my closed eyes. I opened them to a gleaming light. There was my son's smiling face in front of me. I didn't know if I was dreaming or imagining him. Maybe he was really there.

Scott's face had a full moustache and small beard like he had had in his mid-forties. His razor-cut long hair was as fine as *he* was, brown like mine and my mother's. His eyes were glistening and around his neck was the black, leather, single-strand necklace he wore during that time. As in life, he had a serene energy.

"What *now*?" he asked, teasing me, as if I summoned him too often.

"I have some questions for you—pieces of your life I cannot explain. You had so many secrets and kept so much to yourself." I knew this was delicate territory, remembering how he disliked being asked about his feelings.

Scott looked at the orchids he had given me, lining the bay window. His image drifted closer towards my face. "You usually knew how I felt but you didn't want to deal with my pain or hurt feelings. Sure, I was closed down, but you had secrets too," His face had that same naughty look as he'd had when he pulled off a childhood stunt.

We were at that uncomfortable place again, where I felt defensive. He changed the subject. His eyes searched the sky, trees, orchids, and finally back to me. He looked at me square on. It was uncharacteristic. I was mesmerized.

Scott continued, "I'm learning more and more how unconnected and lost I was, always searching for a way to avoid pain or disappointment." He spoke these words but it could have been me saying it too. His gaze did not diminish. I wondered how he could "learn" in the afterlife. I didn't ask, afraid that if I inquired about death, he would simply disappear.

"You were doing just what I did," I said, wanting, as always, to support and forgive him. While on drugs, Scott and I lived a shallow life, empty of genuine honesty. We were unconnected to each other and everyone else, floating in a surreal life, above burdens and reality—of course we fell.

No longer smiling, Scott looked down and said, "I had to escape the pain of my feelings."

"Me too," I went silent. There had been so many similarities in our lives, so much respect we shared. And then it hit me. It was *me* hiding behind a veil or inside another identity, taking on my own secret life of concealment. I tried to reveal myself through art and writing as he had done by dressing up and putting on makeup. My son's image began to fade away.

"Did that help?" he asked. He seemed to be mocking me with his usual kind consideration, dry humor, and lovable smile.

"Yes," I answered as he disappeared into a darkening, magical sky.

* * *

ACCEPTANCE

Losing my son altered my life considerably. In the first years after Scott passed, the only important things were family and friends. I couldn't have maneuvered the aftermath without David—my organized, intelligent, loving husband. My only desire was to run away. Thoughts of travel took over as I searched for B&Bs in exotic places. I sat outside in the backyard as the breeze caressed my face, clouds went by, and nature's noises reminded me that life goes on. I went shopping when I had to. I watched TV, obsessed over news on the internet, and looked for diversions to keep my mind busy.

I tried to make art but hit a wall. Maybe there was too much Scott in my studio? My friend Karen said, "Move it out."

There were boxes of tear-sheets from magazines with photos of the women he made more beautiful, his own artwork, photographs, past collages we made together while working on the Laniege color boards. He was in there, in the walls, in the layers of collages stacked in drawers and on shelves. I saw then how our creativity was linked. Scott's art was inspired by my love of fashion, nature, and glamour. Mine was merged with his love for makeup, astronomy, and beauty.

I became part detective, part archaeologist, and a bit snoop, searching for inspiration and clues about his and my own life—in the papers, magazines, books, and my own past writings about him. Words became messages, directions to make art with meaning when meaning had left me.

I began to combine his image into my abstract paintings as if Scott were still encouraging my collage work. I knew he would not approve of my using his face, but I rejected the critique. I layered his drawings or photos on my art and wrote stories about him. I planned my daily activities around art and writing. This became my therapy. I considered going to a grief counselor but thought my story of us should first be a private one. If I couldn't deal with it, I would reach out for support later.

LOVING SCOTT

I heard something on the radio about going to the edge of the cliff, jumping, and building your wings on the way down. I followed that advice for a time, perceiving that *Scott* had learned to use his wings and was now helping *me*.

Scott in Thailand, c. 1998, UNI

CHAPTER FORTY-SEVEN

COMING OUT OF DENIAL

One day I made my friend cry. It had been a few years since we had last spoken. I told her of Scott's passing and my writing about envisioning him speaking to me. Her daughter had passed away a year before, and I saw how fragile she was. I knew that feeling—the way I had been that first year after Scott passed.

"You never get over losing a child." She told me. It's true. Losing my son *had* changed me. No one expects their child to die before they do. We prepare for floods, storms, sickness, and even poverty, but we don't anticipate losing a child.

Thoughts of death stayed with me for days. My father died when I was sixteen. He had been bedridden for a year and a half, told by the doctor that if he didn't take the new Parkinson's medication, he would only have six months to a year left. He refused to take the drug. My mother and I were aware, every day, that he was living on borrowed time, yet we became hysterical that day. One morning, on a beautiful summer day when I wanted only to be outside working on a tan, I brought my bedridden father soup for lunch and found him dead. He was on his back, with eyes open. I dropped the bowl, ran out sobbing, screaming to my mother. We called the doctor who, knowing my father never took meds, said in disgust, "Why call me? You need to call the undertaker!"

Fifty years later, when I got the call that my son had passed, the same sensations arose—the sickening shock made worse by pretending death would not happen, despite all evidence to the contrary.

Now removed from those deaths by years, I attempted to unpack the facts. I followed hints and tracked incidents like breadcrumbs laid out in a rambled forest. There were obvious symptoms of serious illness: diagnosis of my father's Parkinson's and my son's Hepatitis C, the alcoholism in both men, and Scott's being on the liver transplant list for over a year. *Of course*, he'd not been close to getting the transplant. I should have expected death.

Scott called me months before to ask if I thought he should cash out of his life insurance policy to pay for the thousand-dollars-a-day drug he was to start on. I was named as beneficiary.

"Your health is more important to me." I told him. I hoped that a pill would cure him as I dove back into that locked closet in my head. I wanted to *not* accept reality or the possibility of losing him. I didn't know what else to say or how to act *or* how to deal with it. I pretended everything was normal.

I went on with daily routines: cooking, writing, gardening, attempting to make art, avoiding thinking of dark possibilities. All was light, colorful, shining. I wanted the idea of dying to be far away, under a big rock at the bottom of the ocean. Listening closely to the echoes in my heart that clung to life, I would not read obituaries or be around friends for long who spoke of someone seriously sick. In a daze, I was able to deny the possibility of my own dying or losing someone else I loved. I desired only to live for the present. It was a perfect way to be in reality with just a part of myself.

My poor husband. Years later when I asked how it had been for him during the first years after Scott passed, he said, "It was hard going."

* * *

I sensed the cool air and perceived a slight warming in Scott's embrace.

"It's *not* your fault. I was just ready to go." he whispered.

But I *did* blame myself, my addiction, my mothering. I was on my way to forgiving myself while Scott was content in my memory, sure of himself.

"I want you to be happy, enjoy the rest of your life, don't worry about me," he said. "I did what I wanted to do and accomplished a lot. I learned about love and always loved you even when I was angry. I'm sorry for putting you through the drug years and the last few years when I went back to drinking and drugs. I kept it a secret from you for a long time but just couldn't face losing you. Please forgive me."

I envisioned him speaking to me more than he ever had. Scott was always one of few words, but that day his life poured out of him along with my tears. He wanted me to understand his life was what *he* had made of it, not about me.

He moved closer and sat at the other end of the oversized couch in my bedroom. That was new. In any of my previous visions, I had not imagined him sitting so close to me. That day he was dressed in a light-green sweater with the word *cashmere* in black script on the reverse. He wore this sweater along with his skull ring on the day he was filmed putting makeup on models for three videos for YouTube. I watched the videos until they were no longer available on the web. His hair was pulled back in a ponytail, and he wore glasses and was smiling.

"What are you doing?" he asked me.

"I'm still attempting to conjure you onto this page for posterity," I answered. He laughed again while getting up to look around the room.

"Why aren't you working in your studio?" The image he was looking at was above the side of the bed where I slept—a black and white photograph of a death mask, an unidentified face surrounded by a beige tulle scarf. I had made the collage while living in Paris in 1991 and knew it was the one he had always admired.

"Why write about me when you can do this kind of work?" he asked again, as he had before.

I didn't know how to answer and continued to write. He walked closer to another work, one that had hung in the castle ghost room for many years. It was a requested gift for his birthday, a work I had made in Paris with hand-embroidered lace covering the top and bottom of Edith Piaf's puffy face. Scott pointed to the mask with his long finger.

I told him about buying the book of death masks from a used-bookstore in Paris while thinking of my friend Perry in New York who was dying of AIDS.

Scott moved gazelle-like around the room, studying each artwork. Tall, elegant, so very handsome and engaged on that day, his essence poured out of him. He wanted me to understand him as he approached an abstract work.

"Nice colors and shapes, but what does it *mean*?" he asked.

"Does it have to mean something?" I wondered out loud.

Outside, the sun hid under heavy grey clouds while I attempted to find words that would clarify my abstractions. I became fatigued by this talk about me and my art when I wanted only to focus on him. About to tell him this, I got up and moved to water the orchid, but Scott's image evaporated. Time vanished.

CHAPTER FORTY-EIGHT

BECOMING A PART OF ME

Weeks later, Scott's ghost appeared in the doorway of my bedroom. I was in that dream space as if watching a holographic movie.

"I've been gardening," he said clearly. "Your flowers needed more space. They were disappearing into the shadow, so I separated them." I knew he couldn't really do that. Dressed in the rolled-up khaki pants I was so familiar with and an ethereal, sleeveless, oversized white shirt—he was looking more casual than usual. He drifted closer to me.

"What's up?" he asked as his form floated above me.

"I'm just trying to find the words to explain our relationship," I replied, smiling at him, sitting on the overstuffed couch, writing as the sun flooded in.

"Why waste your time," he muttered as he turned away. It wasn't a question, so I didn't respond as I closed my notebook. We had had this conversation before.

Scott continued. "I'm gone now. Nothing will bring me back."

"I don't believe that!" I told him. "This book will bring you back, if only to me."

Scott was again looking at my art on the wall.

"The death-mask art you created has more life than those dead words. Why did you create it all those years ago, before anyone we knew died—before our world changed?"

I remembered all our friends who died of AIDS and my fears

that my son would join them. How could I answer? Standing up to have a closer look, I reluctantly tried to explain.

"My art and writing were all a search for truth," I responded.

It seemed I was still making things up, ad-libbing more than explaining, a habit from when I was a young mother uncertain how to parent. Now my words felt as obscure as my art, I thought. I wanted to just give up and go garden.

Scott then revealed a deeper truth then he ever had before. "Your actions *did* define me," he said. "Watching you follow your own way, into the reality and fantasy of art, I saw you as more authentic than merely being the way others expected you to be." Scott sat down as tears welled up in my eyes.

"And your approval and support of my dressing up meant a lot to me," he continued as his image transformed into Misty. Now he was wearing an exquisite sequined dress, blue wig, and black eye makeup. His red lips pursed in a cocky expression. I grinned.

Clinging to memories, I was still haunted by critical comments about my son in drag from family and acquaintances during those years of performances and the later photos of Misty published in magazines and books.

"You're now becoming a cultural icon—with your face on sweatshirts and skateboards. How do you feel about that?" I was unhappy seeing my son's image so commercialized.

"I think it's cool," he said, hovering over to pinch off a dried flower from the *Cattleya* orchid he'd given me.

"Look, you grow beautiful flowers but sometimes use them for other things—your art, like when you put a picture of an orchid on a death mask." Turning back to look at me and floating closer, still in drag, Scott set a fuchsia blossom in my hair.

He smiled, "You take life too seriously, Mom, lighten up. All living things die, people die. Everyone becomes memories, or not. Why not make collages like you did after mini-Bush was elected president," Scott advised. "When you had the Statue of Liberty falling into the ocean, while women dressed in black burkas walked towards the sunset."

Scott had always preferred my collages over the abstract paintings, and I understood why he did. Creating a romanticized world was always more fun for Scott than dealing with reality. And abstraction was too far removed from his own authentic narrative. On what came to be one of his last ghostly visits, he merged fantasy with truth.

"Can you join me in the garden?" I asked. My son's phantom form glided towards the door and vanished.

* * *

Summer came early that year as I went off on a quest to find some understanding. Halfway up Guardian Mountain, I rested in a sunny meadow and then saw the deer. She circled me, bobbed her head in curiosity, wary but not afraid. Soon, four more deer came and paused before they ran off. The doe stayed with me, my friend now, as if taking me for granted. I listened to the birds' sweet whistling, crows cawing, and geese honking while the wind gently blew.

The trees looked so alive, each supporting the other through harsh weather, little water, and few nutrients. In a graveyard of dead trees near the top of the mountain, many still stood tall, proud, and beautiful—even long after their lives had ended. Some were young when they died and I wondered what killed them. As they fed the forest and insects, the trees seemed to live again by sustaining other life. They have much to teach us.

Everything seemed a mystery as I forgot more than I remembered. My soul was in despair, but when I felt Scott's hand on my shoulder, I wasn't alone anymore.

Scott at castle, c. 2005 PA

EPILOGUE

LOOKING BACK

My son grew tall, with straight posture. He walked like a prince with head held high while moving gracefully with dramatic dignity. He had a beautiful, gentle face with perfect bone structure, a classical Greek nose, and piercing dark eyes that looked deeply into others' faces, connecting to each soul and heart. With his long hair he made both women and men admire his charming androgyny.

Despite his beauty, Scott had a weakness for drugs and alcohol, as I did. Through thorough searching, I examined old secrets and surfaced with the cause of his starting drugs at an early age. There were gaps in my memory during the seventies and early eighties under the fog of alcohol. Rereading my journals gave me startling indications of my character. Regardless that I loved my children and thought I was a good mother and friend to them, I know now it was simply a disguise I wore. I naïvely assumed my kids were strong enough to not pattern themselves after me.

When Scott was young, I was emotionally unavailable, numb, or angry on most days. I believed I had passed my addiction, and my father's, onto him. In my journals, I put the fault on *his* father or whatever boyfriend I had at the time. I blamed Scott's friends, his school, even New York City. But the real reason Scott did drugs, got Hep C, and returned to drinking after almost twenty-five years of sobriety was due to an addiction that got the better of him, an addiction he saw in me.

Scott could have died alone in his basement apartment in 1986, when I brought him food and pleaded with him to stop doing drugs. We held interventions with family and those who loved him, without which he would likely have overdosed then and there, or when he was hooked on Oxycontin for back pain at the castle years later. My most profound joy was sharing more than twenty years with him while he was clean and sober.

I had planned to see him in the city a week before he died and still regret not having made the time. Do all mothers feel guilt and remorse? How many secrets are kept about our siblings, sons, daughters, and friends—when we could be doing *something* to address addiction and social problems out loud?

Today I no longer need drugs or alcohol to escape from my own issues and the chaos and circus atmosphere of the world where all was once too much yet never enough. I continually search for forgiveness and understanding, both for myself and those I love.

It helps to look at things I did right: thirty-five years of sobriety, art I created, encouraging Scott's accomplishments of beauty, intelligence, independence, and self-reliance. I hope I had a part in that and honor the trials we went through and the love we shared.

I hear echoes of vague, hazy memories, while Scott—as a ghost now—drifts with me. He joins me in dreams where our spirits float together, communicating, celebrating the love and admiration we had for each other over fifty years. He is part of me now, and will still be part of my future, near me, a comforting companion. Our love feels eternal.

My own reality is a place not quite as magical as my imagination. I want more than these memories and words on paper. I long to be in this life as well as in a dreamscape where I am not dead but can converse with the dead. Where I can again feel the strong arms of my son hugging me tightly and kissing me, a soft kiss I would never wipe off.

EPILOGUE: LOOKING BACK

I eventually progressed through locked gates of past truths. And yet, self-recrimination remained an obstinate floating vapor trail as I wrote. It reached out like delicate ghost limbs, trying to lift a veil off of me. Darkness was my shadow as I wrote in a dazed condition. At times I lost hold of my own awareness. I fumbled with the key to unlock that door.

My shame and grief mirrored each other. I used distractions to keep them at bay. At times, I watched TV news incessantly, as if my anger from bad events could prevent me from feeling all the other negative emotions.

I employed any effort of obstruction or denial to cover up the fact that Scott was gone forever. The anger *did* pull me out of being stuck, though memories of him were fading, and I feared that loss. I wondered if my remorse would ease at the completion of this book.

I have come to accept death yet still fear the grief it brings. I check the breath of my husband some nights and make sure to call my brother and sister every few weeks. I drive extra carefully and take time to listen more to friends and elders as much as possible.

My sister Nancy recently asked, "Do you ever think maybe you don't want to finish the book on Scott?" Her insight struck me by surprise. I never suspected that as a possibility. Speechless, I looked down at the floor, pondering the idea. Perhaps she was right. Then it hit me how hard I had been holding on.

Whatever was in this bit of truth from my sister was attached to my inability to move forward. I searched through fragmented memories and became overwhelmed. Confused, I shut doors I wanted to open. I even welcomed the ache. It became my safe place.

My favorite French philosopher Michel de Montaigne wrote, "Nothing fixes a thing so intensely in the memory as the wish to forget it." I no longer tried to forget yet knew it was time to let go.

When I look at the sky or watch the sun dappling on green

grass, I imagine Scott inside a better part of my heart. He speaks to me, and I'm filled with love. The shadows go away as light finds its way in.

* * *

There is a swinging redwood bench under the large red maple tree by the stream in back of our house in Willow. Scott often went directly to that bench when he visited. He would sit alone until I joined him.

"How's everything going?" I asked.

"Fine," he answered. After a bit of small talk, we sat in silent memories—swinging together gently, back and forth, listening to the water rush by. It was our way to connect without the chaos of the world intruding.

When pouring Scott's ashes in the urn at his gravesite, I saved a cupful in a small Chinese ceramic pot Scott had given me from one of his Asian trips. The top cover is a foo dog head with a smile and mustache. He told me it symbolized protection. I promised myself I would scatter the remainder of his ashes near the bench, in the stream.

But first, the largest *Cattleya labiata* orchid Scott gave me twelve years ago needed watering. The plant has four buds on it this year. *Cattleyas* are known as "Queen of the orchids" and when they blossom, the delicate petals become a pale lavender through rich shades of pink and crimson, the deep ruby inclining to purple. Each of the four flowers on the plant would be seven inches across. *Cattleyas* have a spicy floral scent that evokes the rainforests of Brazil, where they were first discovered. The orchid reminds me of Scott.

I filled a pitcher and carefully watered the bark underneath the buds, just a bit, enough for them to bloom, in time.

Scott's friends at his memorial in NYC, 2014,
PA

One of Scott's last makeup jobs, NYC. 2014,
Photo by Christian Ferretti

ACKNOWLEDGMENTS AND CREDITS

I am indebted to the many supporters, writers and readers who offered encouragement and advice along this path. My husband David Ekroth for endless editing; Nancy Kline and participants of the Woodstock Library Poets and Writers Workshop; Martha Hughes and Maureen brady and participants from the Paripatetic Writing Workshop; Marlene Adelstein, for her excellent book doctoring; Craig Mahwirt for tireless reading and editing; Jana Martin, Violet Snow, Elin Menzies, Lauri Heaven and Mernie Buchanan, mentors with sound guidance and the many other friends and family who kindly read early drafts. Gratitude to Colin Rolfe and Dory Mayo from Epigraph Publishing for their support and counsel.

Thanks to Nan Goldin, Linda Simpson, David Armstrong, Serge Normant, Sebastien Richard, Jed Root, Michael Thompson and the hundreds of photographers who recorded Scott in and out of drag and/or his makeup art on models and female or male actors.

Photographs with PA indicates photo by author, Pat Horner.

UNI indicates photographer unknown.

The provenance of many images remains uncertain. If discovered, attribution can be made in future editions.

ABOUT THE AUTHOR

Pat Horner first published at age sixteen with her column, Horner's Corner, in the Minneapolis Central High newspaper. She went on to become a photographer, collage artist, abstract painter, writer, journalist, teacher, and creative coach. Her stories, articles, and art have been published in *Utne Reader*, *The Progressive*, *Woodstock Times*, *Blue Stocking*, *Inside/Out*, and *Wildlife Art* magazines.

When her son, Scott, passed away in 2014, Pat embarked on a quest to explore their passionate fifty years of joy, sorrow, and fabulous makeup. Horner lives in Woodstock, New York, with her husband, David.